8 reasons why i'm not a christian.

8 reasons why i'm not a christian.
Myths and Misconceptions

Copyright © 2011 Published by Word of Life Fellowship, Inc.
P.O. Box 600
Schroon Lake, Ny 12870

www.wol.org

Please note: The authors have prepared a DVD video series to accompany this text. Information regarding the series is available is found in the back of this book.

Cover design by
ISBN: 978-1-935475-19-4

www.8reason.wol.org

Printed in the United States of America

Contents

chapter 1

Christianity Does Not Work
Ric Garland

When we're looking at common objections to Christianity, the most obvious objection is: Christianity flat-out doesn't work.

Christianity may be a good tool to get people to be nice to each other or a way for church leaders and parents to show they're in charge, but for you, it doesn't work. It doesn't have any power for you; it doesn't change your life. The rules, rituals, and habits of Christianity aren't anything special, and often they just cause more trouble.

Now, you may be right. Christianity may not work—for you. But that is because you're approaching it differently than it was intended.

I suggest it this way: You need to change your religion to a relationship.

Wait! I know you're already shaking your head, flipping the page. You've heard this so many times. If you've been raised in the church, you've been told this is what separates you from the other religions and belief systems out there.

You wonder how your life and the way you've been indoctrinated is different from the Buddhist kid halfway around the globe. You question how the Jesus you're supposed to "know" is different from the Jesus your Catholic friends know.

Even if you haven't been in the church your whole life, you realize there's a disconnect when people say Christianity is a relationship, but so much of what Christians do looks very much like religion.

But give me a minute. Let's see if we can get beyond the phrases you've always heard about "relationship, not religion" and get to what it really means to know this God, your Savior, the One Who gives you a different life than the millions who follow religions around the world.

If you've never heard that Christianity is supposed to be a relationship, this will help you, too. I want to show you that the main reason why Christianity doesn't "work"—for you, and even for people that have been in the faith for many years—is because most of the time we approach it the wrong way.

Let's start with the difference between "religion" and "relationship." You know what relationships are; you have them, good or bad, with your family and your friends. You're also familiar with religions, which basically focus on what people can do to find their way to God. Religious practices like becoming one with nature, getting in touch with an outer spirit, being good to others—these all involve something we have to do to get to God.

You see, religion is about how man gets to God, but Christianity is about how God came to man. Do you see the difference?

Paul explained it this way: "For it isn't the cutting of our bodies that makes us children of God; it is worshiping Him with spirit." Paul talks about this "cutting of the body" —the Jewish practice of circumcision— in Philippians 3:3: "For we are the circumcision, who worship God in the Spirit, rejoice in Christ Jesus, and have no confidence in the flesh."

What Paul is saying is that it's not the things we do—practicing circumcision or the other works that may be associated with religion— that define Christianity; it's our connection to Jesus Christ.

As Christians, we glory in what Christ Jesus has done for us and realize that we are helpless to save ourselves. It's not about what we ourselves do to make religion work, because we will never make it work enough to satisfy our souls. It's about what He has done for us.

Jesus Christ came and died on the cross for our sin—He came to us. He was buried and rose again, and our faith is about putting our trust in Him. We trust that His act and His righteousness can change us. He wants a relationship with us.

He doesn't want us working our way to Him; He wants to extend Himself to us. Do you see the difference?

What about the stuff that doesn't make sense? The Bible has answers for that, and God explains how this out-of-control world fits with His reaching out to us and saving us. But we need to start at the right place. Rather than worrying about circumstances and the way the world looks, let's make sure we fully understand what it means to have a real relationship with God. Everything else comes after that. We need to make sure we know what this relationship looks like, that we aren't just saying the phrase while still living out a religion.

The tricky thing with Christianity is that a lot of people treat it as a religion. For some it's a relationship, but often both perspectives look the same from the outside. We may think we're treating it as a relationship, because that's what people call it, but really we're still pushing religion—trying to get to God.

Relationship stops that. We're not trying to *get to* God. We're just focusing on Him.

So, what do you need to do?

You need to deny. What do I mean by deny? I mean this: We need to humble ourselves, deny that we have anything to do with changing ourselves. Let's stop making it about us, and make it about God. He wants a relationship with you. He's done all the work—you just need to receive the gift He wants to give you.

I find that this is so difficult for people. We all understand that we are sinners. We all understand that Jesus died and rose again. But you know what the difficult part is? It's hard for us to humble ourselves and say, "I'm going to admit it—I can't do it."

Until we admit that even if we are really good, and really talented, and try really hard to reach God, we cannot—we'll never get to Him. There's no "halfway" here. We need to humble ourselves and admit that no one but God can get us where we need to be.

Do you know what the **second** thing is you have to change? **You've got to be willing to die instead of dominate.**

This is part of what happens at salvation, and then it continues after we are saved. We know we're sinners, but we can't just admit that and then think we'll start cleaning ourselves up once we say we believe Jesus died and rose again. We have to die.

You may wonder what I mean. You may think, "Now that I'm a Christian, I'm going to fix my life. I'm going to do what I want to do. I'm going to work on being nice and figure out where I'm going to serve. I'm going to tell God what I'm going to give to Him and what I'll hold back."

Look at Philippians 3:10: "That I may know Him and the power of His resurrection." That Greek word for "power" means *to overcome resistance.* Jerry Bridges says it this way: "Our first problem is that our attitude toward sin is more self-centered than God-centered. We are more concerned about our own victory over sin than we are about the fact that sin grieved the heart of God. We cannot tolerate failure in our struggle with sin chiefly because we are success-oriented and not because we know that it is offensive to God."

You see, when we try to "work on" our lives or get rid of certain sins, the focus is coming back to us. We're trying to reach God rather than seeking what *He* wants to do for us. That's why we need to die— to give up, to stop feeding our working side—if we want to see Him overcome the power of sin in our lives. He didn't save us so we could start trying to improve ourselves again.

There's a story of a missionary in Africa some years ago. He had a jeep, a wife, and a little daughter. One morning they were getting ready to go somewhere in the jeep. Apparently during the night a very poisonous snake had crawled up in the jeep to lay on the warm engine. The missionary turned on the jeep, and when he cranked it up, the snake dropped down right in front of his feet. It reared back and bit him, and it reared back so quickly that it bit the little baby also. The baby was only three months old. The natives were horrified because the snake was a deadly one. There was no cure in the area, and they said the baby would die. The baby's legs started to swell up. Minutes went by, then hours. The swelling moved up the legs. Then, hours later, the swelling started going back down again. A day later the baby was fine.

Remember how I told you that before the snake bit the baby, it bit the missionary? The missionary was wearing cowboy boots, and when the snake bit into the leather of the cowboy boot, its fangs never penetrated the skin. But in doing so, it extracted out all its venom. So when it bit the little baby, there was no venom left.

Ladies and gentlemen, listen to me: Satan cannot have power over you. As a believer, Jesus has taken all the venom out of Satan for you.

You and I need to die. We need to say, "I'm going to die." We need to put to death that side of us that is living and fighting and trying to work so hard. God is the only One Who can give us success in our fight against sin. We must deny ourselves and say, "Yes, I have come to know Christ as Savior. I'm going to now die and say, 'God, dominate my life. Come in and change me.'"

Look over these verses in Philippians 3. Paul wanted to experience the power that resurrected Jesus from the dead; he wanted that power to surge through his life, to overcome sin in his life so great things could be done for God. He needed to die, and we need to die.

The third thing you need to do is make a decision instead of living a double life. You need to make up your mind. Look at verse 10: "That I may know Him and the power of His resurrection, and the fellowship of His sufferings." I don't think this context is talking about when Jesus suffered before He died on the cross. In context, Paul is talking about suffering for being misunderstood. He's not saying, "Get a grip on how much physical pain Jesus went through." He's saying, "I want to understand the life Jesus lived on this earth." The Christian life leaves so many opportunities for us to be misunderstood. People may not get why we do certain things, or maybe why we're so focused on dying to self and being humbled! Many people do not understand God's truth.

Are you willing to suffer for being misunderstood? Jesus Christ is asking, "Hey, are you willing to be identified with Me?"

Jesus had four half-brothers and at least two half-sisters, and not one of them believed He was the Messiah until after He was resurrected from the dead. Talk about a dysfunctional family! The Gospels are full of stories of people rejecting Jesus and the way He looked at the world. He suffered for us, and He was misunderstood. None of that mattered to Him because He knew He was doing what God wanted. His focus was on God.

You and I need to make a decision. Must of us genuinely love God, but we are looking for a way to live that allows us to mix our love for God with our love for the world. You may think you're not doing that, but let me ask you this—do you ever try to find a way to squish your Christian beliefs into your everyday life? Do you try to make your faith look inoffensive? Maybe you think you should be able to live your Christian life in a way that won't upset anyone. Or maybe you think that you can do worldly things without changing your Christian lifestyle. But the Bible has plenty of verses that suggest otherwise. God's Word says the world and Christianity don't mix. And the longer you try to make them mix, you'll see that one has to go—or neither will work. You just can't do it. It won't work.

We tend to live under two agendas: ours and God's. The tension between the two is what creates stress. Do you have stress in your life? Here's what you have to do: Remove an agenda. I would suggest yours, because God's is not going anywhere. You need to decide that you will live by faith and believe Him.

The fourth thing you need to change is your beliefs, not your behavior. This may surprise you. Isn't the whole point of Christianity that we're changing?

You say, "You're not interested in me changing my behavior, where I'm going, and what I'm doing?" No. My point is found in Scripture. Verse 10 says "being conformed to His death." Do you know what "being conformed" means? It means *giving out expression to intrinsic nature*. Or, in normal people words, it means a way of living that shows what's going on inside.

Here's what I want you to do: Change your belief system. You won't have to worry about your behavior. The new belief system will have an effect.

What do I mean by "change your belief system"? Discipline your life. Now, what is discipline? Discipline is getting in the Word of God, having a time of daily devotions, and memorizing Scripture. If you start reading, and believing, and applying this Book to your life, you won't have to worry about your behavior. It's going to change, because the Bible is going to change your beliefs.

Now, you may think, "You told me not to change my behavior, but now you're telling me to *do* something—what is that all about?" Discipline is very different from you going out there and trying to change your behavior. When you focus on your behavior, you're going to come across choices that confuse you, and you're going to run out of strength. But discipline is different. It's changing your mind. It's putting the correct beliefs and attitudes in your mind so that God can work. Yes, you need to "do" things to practice disciplines, but these won't do you any good on their own—the truth you are learning and the God behind it are the difference!

Philippians 3:10 is talking about the dynamic life Paul wants us to experience. When we *know* God through His Word (getting to know Him, as in a relationship), we find power to overcome sin and confidence to endure suffering. In doing this, we become more like Christ. This is real, authentic, genuine Christianity. But you have to deny, die, decide, and then discipline to see God's power work, to see this relationship become real. There are three different ways you can go with this. You can believe the myth. You know what the myth is? The myth is that Christianity doesn't work. The myth is that Christianity is just like every other religion out there.

Or you can believe the misconception. The misconception is that you need to work backward. You may have tried to work backward. You say, "I'm going to discipline my life first. I'm going to try to go to church faithfully. I'm going to try to do good works. I'm going to try not to say the bad words. I'm going to try all these things, and then I'll decide whether I want Christ. Then I'll decide whether I die. Then finally, I'll die." You have it all backward.

You may read stories about great "heroes of the faith" and see the different things they did and think, "OK, if I do those things, I'll make progress." But you have to realize that those things came *after* their relationship with God. God was doing the work; they were just making the space for Him to work.

You may be a Christian already, but all you can look at are the disciplines. In fact, all you're doing is choking on the disciplines because you haven't started with saying, "OK God, I've already denied and said I want You as my Savior," but you haven't died to yourself. The disciplines are no good without the death. Maybe you even think that by doing the disciplines, you're going to eventually get to dying in Christ—enough good stuff will bring transformation. That is backward.

Of course there is a third way you can do this. Are you going to believe the truth? You may have heard the Gospel, but you've said, "Man, I haven't bought into it." I want you to know that it does work. It works, but it only works one way. God's way. God has only one way. Now, be careful about what you've heard about "God's way." Some people think this means everything will be fine, that you'll have utopia on earth. They say God gives everyone a car or keeps them from being sick. They say you'll always be happy. That's not what God promises though. There is no utopia here on earth. God doesn't promise that you won't have any problems. If you come into Christianity and receive Christ as your Savior, it doesn't take care of every problem. God never promised that.

Here's what He did promise, and it's better than things going well here on earth for a while: Your sins are forgiven, and you'll have a relationship with God and a home in Heaven forever. That is what He promised.

You may have tried it your own way, but you realize it doesn't work because you have it all wrong. It doesn't work your way. It only works one way, and that's God's way.

Would you come to know Jesus Christ as your personal Savior? Just say, "I admit that I'm a sinner. I realize that I can't fix it." All you have to do is receive the free gift of eternal life through Jesus Christ.

Now, I want to talk to those of you who are saved. Maybe you're reading this and you know Jesus Christ as your Savior. You have come to the point where you have humbled yourself and denied yourself and have come to Jesus Christ and asked Him to be your Savior. But you're reading this and thinking, "Man, it's not working for me." It's not working because you have done it all backward and you have done it all wrong. You say, "Man, I tried to go to church, I tried to read my Bible and do my quiet time. I tried to do the stuff, but it doesn't work." May I ask you a question? Have you ever died to yourself? Did you ever say, "God, I know that You died for me and You saved me from the penalty of sin, but God, I still have a hold of my life. I need to die to myself, and I want You to conquer the power of sin in my life." Maybe you're reading this and you realize you have to decide. You are living your life in this world. You have one foot over here and one foot over there, and you're trying to customize your Christianity. I want you to know that God never intended Christianity to be customized. He says, "I want you to live this way." He's not being tough—He's actually being loving, because if you do it His way, it's incredible. It will make a difference in your life.

So, do you know Jesus Christ as your Savior? May I suggest that it does work? Would you be willing to call on His name today and be saved?

If you're reading this and you are saved, but you're struggling with it not working in your life, are you willing to die? Would you be willing to decide? Then discipline your life and see great things happen for God.

You have a choice.

God Does Not Care
Mike Calhoun

I think one of the most important things that you and I can realize is that God does care.

A common objection to Christianity is that God doesn't really care. You may hear this from people who have rejected the Gospel, or from those who say the Christian God doesn't make sense logically—that bad things wouldn't happen if He really cared. A lot of people point to the pain and suffering in the world—the cancer, the abuse, the hunger—as evidence that God doesn't care.

Even Christians wonder if God cares. Now, a lot of people are afraid to say this out loud—you're afraid you'll get zapped if you say something like that—but deep down, that's how you feel. You know all these truths about God, and you know He's supposed to care, but in your personal life, you're just not sure He does.

One of the most important things to realize is that God does care.

What I would like for us to do is look at some Biblical examples. When we think of people that say God doesn't care, a lot of times we imagine those people are far away from God. In actuality, it's people right from the pages of Scripture. What I want to do is help us understand something: a lot of people feel God isn't there, that He doesn't remember them, and that He has abandoned them.

Look at these people in Scripture. In Judges 6:13 God is calling Gideon. "Gideon said to Him, 'O my Lord, if the LORD is with us, why then has all this happened to us? And where are all His miracles which our fathers told us about, saying, 'Did not the LORD bring us up from Egypt?' But now the LORD has forsaken us and delivered us into the hands of the Midianites.'"

God was saying to Gideon, "I want you to rescue your nation. I want to use you." Gideon basically looked at Him and said, "If You want me to do this and You are God, then why did all this happen? I don't get it. Where were you?"

Jeremiah, in Lamentations 5:20, said, "Why do You forget us forever, and forsake us for so long a time?" So here is Jeremiah, one of the great prophets of God, and he's writing, "Hey God, did you forget about us?"

Ezekiel 8:6: "Furthermore He said to me, 'Son of man, do you see what they are doing, the great abominations that the house of Israel commits here, to make Me go far away from My sanctuary? Now turn again, you will see greater abominations." Ezekiel goes on to talk about all the things going on in the people's lives and how terrible they are. He asks, "God, can't You see what's happening? Don't You see what we're dealing with every day?"

Now these are questions asked by people, by the way, who were people of God. They were people who really loved God. These people were being used for God in great ways, for specific purposes, yet they still struggled with this.

What about Daniel? We read about him all the way throughout the book of Daniel, and we read about how incredible he was, how he stood up for his faith, and how he wouldn't just give in and cave to the world. Now you come into his life, after all the things that have happened to him, and you come to chapter 6, and you find that he's been tricked. The leaders of that day didn't like him. They didn't like the fact that he was standing for Christ or standing for his faith. So they got with the king and had him sign a decree that if anyone prayed to anyone else but him, they would be thrown in a lions' den. Sure enough, Daniel was still true to God. He went and prayed, and he got in trouble for it.

Daniel could have very well said something like, "Hey God, I have been walking with you, I have been living for you, I have been doing all those things, and You're going to let these evil people hurt me now?" It doesn't fit—there's a disconnect here. People living for God and following Him shouldn't be the ones getting in trouble, right?

How about David? The man after God's own heart—one of Israel's greatest leaders? In Psalm 10:1 he asks, "Why do You stand afar off, O LORD? Why do You hide in times of trouble?" He is literally asking, "Why are you so far away from me?" Again the psalmist writes in Psalm 13:1, "How long, O LORD? Will You forget me forever? How long will You hide Your face from me?" We think sometimes that the only people who think like that are those of us living in modern society. Not so. David is asking, "Why did you forget me, God?"

Another time in the Psalms, Psalm 13:2, he asks, "How long shall I take counsel in my soul, Having sorrow in my heart daily? How long will my enemy be exalted over me?" He asks, "Lord, how long do I have to feel bad like I do and the evil people just get to feel good?" It doesn't make sense. Here you are, going to school, living for God, doing what you are supposed to do, and there's difficulty in your life. These people that are turning against God, they just seem to be doing so well. Disconnect.

Maybe Psalm 42:3: "My tears have been my food day and night, while they continually say to me, 'Where is your God?'" He's talking about other people asking him where His God is. Perhaps you've tried to share your faith and someone said they don't even think there is a God. They challenge you, where's God?

Even Psalm 22, which is penned about Jesus Christ, foretelling His death on the cross, asks these questions. In Psalm 22:1, it says, as Jesus would say later, "My God, My God, why have You forsaken Me? Why are You so far from helping Me, and from the words of My groaning?"

You may know it better from Matthew 27:46, as Jesus is hanging on the cross. Here He is, the Son of God, and He cries out to God: "My God, My God, why have You forsaken Me?"

You may say, "OK, wait a minute. You're supposed to be giving me encouragement. You're supposed to be helping me. You're supposed to be pointing me in the right direction, but what you're saying is what I hear every day. What you're saying is what the people say to me when I try to tell them that God loves them."

Understand something: Feelings are so strong, and many of us live by our feelings, but we have to move from our feelings to something that we know. One of the great issues of dealing with questions like this is getting to that point of something solid—past our feelings, into something we know is true.

The first thing we need to realize is that we have such a small perspective on life. We could talk about God being infinite, and that we are finite. He has no limits and we do. But that doesn't help answer the questions about these feelings that God's not there.

What happens many times is you are faced with a question, and someone says to you, "If God really cares, why is He silent? If God really cares, why does this happen? If God really cares, then why is He not coming to my rescue?" One of the things we have to do is help this person see the big picture. Here's the thing we have to understand: It's really not about us. It's really not about you. It's not about your crisis, it's not about your moment, it's not about that feeling. It's bigger than that. When we ask these questions, the emphasis is on "me" and what's happening to "us," but often we forget to look at the other side, to think about God. I want to go back through some of the verses we talked about earlier and show you the big picture, if I could.

For example, we talked about Gideon. Gideon, in Judges 6, says, "Hey God, if you really are God, and You're going to deliver us from the Midianites, then I have a question for you. Why did you let all these things happen? Where have you been?" It's an honest question, a straightforward question. But all of a sudden now, as we move through this particular book of Judges and we follow the story of Gideon in chapter 7, here's what we begin to find. We begin to see God's bigger picture. God had allowed the Midianites to persecute the people of Israel, to hold them in slavery and hurt them, because the people of Israel had chosen their own way. They had sinned, and God had used the Midianites to bring retribution so they would turn around.. God took this man with 300 soldiers, and they went up against the Midianites, who had 135,000 soldiers. If you do quick math, that's 450 to 1. So, here they are, 450 to 1, and they're going to go down and destroy the Midianites.

Now understand something—the Midianites were warring people. These were like the Green Beret guys—they were really tough. The people of Israel, on the other hand, were farmers who only fought to protect themselves. So God takes these 300 farmers and says, "Go get 'em."

Let's add a little bit more to the dynamic of this story. You know what they had for a weapon? They had a clay pitcher, a torch, and a trumpet. You go, "I would want a bazooka, a tank or something. Let's get some air strikes in here. I need a little bit of help." But God gave them these weapons and performed a miracle through them. They just had to get the big picture of what God was doing.

What about the story we read in Lamentations 5? Do you remember what Jeremiah said? "God, did you forget about us?" If you look in Lamentations 3, Jeremiah says, "I called on Your name, O Lord, from the lowest pit, and you heard my voice. ... You didn't hide from me. You didn't hide from my crying. You drew near to me when I called on You, and You said, 'Don't be afraid.'"

Jeremiah needed to realize that he had to get to that place in his life where he would call upon God. See, one of the issues we face is that we are so full of ourselves. I am, you are, we are all so full of ourselves. Many times we want to be dependent on God, but we keep relying on ourselves. Then something comes into our life and blows things apart and we realize, "I have nowhere to go but to God."

Let's think through those passages in Ezekiel. Ezekiel said, "God, can't You see what's happening? I mean, don't You understand?" God answers him in chapter 18, verse 23: "'Do I have any pleasure at all that the wicked should die?' says the Lord GOD, 'and not that he should turn from his ways and live?'" He says, "I don't have any pleasure in seeing the wicked die, but they have to wake up!" He goes on to say, "I'm not really excited to see the people who know Me turn and go the wrong direction." What is the answer here? God is saying, "Look, I see all this, but I want you to know something. I have a plan, even for the wicked."

That's tough for us to understand. It's hard to see that God has a plan that is bigger than us.

In Daniel chapter 6, the leaders say, "King, are you going to be true to your word and have Daniel thrown in the lions' den?" They threw him in, but when the king went to check on Daniel, here's what happened. Daniel 6:20 says, "And when he came to the den, he cried out with a lamenting voice to Daniel. The king spoke, saying to Daniel, 'Daniel, servant of the living God, has your God, whom you serve continually, been able to deliver you from the lions?'" Daniel must have made a pretty strong impression. The king knew about his God. He also said, "Whom thou servest continually." Man, what a great testimony.

The king finds out that, yes, God had delivered Daniel. God allowed the situation to prove that His servant Daniel was true. He allowed the situation to prove His power; He allowed the situation to teach a king. He allowed the situation to turn a nation to Him. He allowed the situation to punish the wicked. Now we can see the big picture. Most of us only get the micro vision; we can't see everything.

Remember the passage we looked at in Psalm 10:1? "Why are you so far from me?" the psalmist asks. God says, "I'm not very far." Psalm 139:7 reads, "Where can I go from Your Spirit? Or where can I flee from Your presence?" We know that one of the attributes of God is that He's everywhere, so there's nowhere we can go where he is not there. The psalmist knows He has to be there, so he cries out, "Where are You? I feel like You're far off."

What about Psalm 13? David asks, "Did you forget about me?" A little bit later we find out that not only did God not forget about David, but He also delivered him. In Psalm 18:1–2, David says, "I will love You, O LORD, my strength. The LORD is my rock and my fortress and my deliverer; My God, my strength, in whom I will trust; My shield and the horn of my salvation, my stronghold." David spoke these words the day God delivered him. After all that crying out and reciting God's promises back to Him, God came through.

David goes on to say, "I will love You, O LORD, my strength. The LORD is my rock and my fortress and my deliverer; My God, my strength, in whom I will trust; My shield and the horn of my salvation, my stronghold." We go from a point where David is melancholy and says, "Wait a minute God, did you forget about me?" to the point where all of a sudden he realizes that God really is his stronghold. God is the Anchor of his soul.

God was always the Anchor of his life, but David lost his perspective.

When you think about the truth of the Word of God, understand something. This is not about God in the sense that there's a question about Him. It's about us and our discovery of Him—coming to the place of discovering Who He really is.

Who God is and whether He's there doesn't change. What has been adjusted is where we come in. In Psalm 42:11, David comes back and says, "Look, put your hope in God; put your trust in Him because He will take care of you." In Psalm 22 and Matthew 27, remember Jesus' question: "My God, My God, why have You forsaken Me?" If you follow that passage from Psalm 22 verse 1 to verse 27, it says, "All the end of the world shall remember and turn to the Lord...."

My friend, understand something, Jesus Christ died on the cross. For that moment, it looked pretty bleak. But this was part of the big picture—the plan of God that He would be glorified and that people like you and me would be able to come to Him and know Him as personal Savior.

Sometimes we forget who really is in control. I talk to people about their faith and I say, "Hey, do you know Jesus Christ as your Savior?" They say, "No, I don't want to be a Christian." I say, "Why don't you want to be a Christian?" They say, "Because I just want to live my own life. I'm doing my own thing. I don't need God." How deceived are we, to think that we are in charge, that we are the ones making the decisions? What we get down to is this: We have to come to a place in our lives where we decide if we're going to trust the truth.

We may think we can change things, that we can be in control, but the truth is that God is in control. Scripture is very clear that He knows what's going on, that He's aware of each of our lives, and that He's controlling them. That's a tough thought when we think about some of the tragedy and some of the crises that are happening right now. But we need to trust the truth. Is God really in control? We have to get to a place where we are willing to accept the truth as a matter of faith. I don't understand, but I trust.

Go back to Daniel. He had to say, "God, I don't understand, I'm living right, and something doesn't make sense." The psalmist says, "I'm trying to serve You, and it doesn't make sense." Jeremiah says, "Here I am preaching and teaching. The people are trying to turn, and it doesn't make sense."

There are myths and misconceptions about Christianity that cause us to ask questions. The myth goes like this: "God doesn't care; God has just totally forgotten about me." It's easy for us to believe that, particularly if you are going through a hard time, particularly if you've had a crisis of faith. Some of you are at a stage of life right now where you have been living on borrowed faith, if you will. You've been living on the fact that your parents are Christians or you're in a church or whatever, but you've never really quite made it your own. As you begin to make it your own, if you're not careful, you're going to find yourself following the myth. You're going to find that your head is so full of all this Christian information and all these truths, but because you haven't made it your own, you're not grasping that God really does care. There's a God behind all these circumstances, and He wants a relationship with you. But until you seek this God, it will be very difficult to overcome the myth that He doesn't care.

There's a misconception too. The misconception goes something like this: Since God really doesn't care about people, and we're all we've got, we've got to take care of ourselves. We find people getting involved in aid for this and an aid for that. I think that is all good—it's good to support each other and take care of each other. But understand this: If all we do is take care of this body, we're in trouble, because we are more than a body. We may be able to take care of ourselves physically, or look out for each other a little bit, but we're missing the parts that only God can take care of. We unite and have our groups here and our societies there. We think, "We'll just make up for the fact that there is no God, or that He's distant, or that He's forgotten, or that He just doesn't really care." But no matter how much we try to make up for God with our communities or our causes, it's not going to be enough.

You have to make a decision. You have to come to a place where you think either it's a myth or a misconception, or you're going to come to a place where you accept the truth. I have not tried to coerce you into believing the truth. I simply showed you some illustrations from Scripture about some very valid people who loved God but struggled with some of the very same questions. Not until they got to the point of seeing the big picture could they comprehend what was really going on in their lives. We have to do the same thing—we have to come to the truth, to see the big picture.

Here is an interesting verse. Isaiah 45:7 says, "I form the light and create darkness, I bring prosperity and create disaster; I, the LORD, do all these things." God is speaking, and He says He forms the light and creates the darkness. We are all good with that. He says, "I make peace." OK, we're all good, but here's the next part: "And create calamity." He says, "I create the light, and the dark, and also the calamity." In other words, "I make peace, but I also bring about crisis and strife." You go, "OK, wait a minute. Now you're really messing with my mind." He goes on to say, "I, the Lord, do all these things."

See the truth is this—this is not about you; this is not about me. This is about God. We have to quit making excuses for God. We have to get to the point of realizing, "You know what? He is God. He is the Creator of the universe, and He can do whatever He wants to do." That really bothers some people. They look at Him and say, "Well, He's just an arrogant God. He's up there trying to do all these things."

He created the universe, so He knows the big picture. I'm not saying that God throws all these terrible things at us. I'm not saying He brings the tsunamis. But I am saying this: He's the very same God that controls everything, and He could control that.

What we like to do is crawl inside of our little Christian cocoon and say, "Our God is just a loving God, and He would never do that. That's only because of this." We make excuses for why God would do certain things because maybe we're not ready to embrace the truth of Who God is.

Maybe we're also afraid to look at the truth of who we are. Because of the free will of man, because we have a choice, these things happen. The reason these things happen around the world, when you trace them back, is because of the choice of man. You say, "Well, wait a minute. People don't cause earthquakes or tsunamis, and so on." You are correct, they are not the direct cause but the sin of mankind nevertheless is to blame. The world is in an unhappy state because of our sin.

We have to come to a place where we realize that God is God. That doesn't mean that we are puppets, because we do have free will. In Joshua 24, Joshua cries out in verse 15, "Choose for yourselves this day whom you will serve." We have a choice. We can make a decision.

You talk about some reasons why you don't want to become a Christian. That's a choice. But understand God has a bigger plan. It's not just about you, and it's not just about this moment. You have a freedom of choice. You can feel all you want that God doesn't care or that He's not in control, but that is your choice. And when you choose that, you're denying the truth of the Bible. I understand people's concerns; it's a valid objection to Christianity to question whether God cares—until we look at the Word and see that He does care. Then it's our choice to accept it or not.

We think we are in control because it really looks like that. Think about a cruise ship going from Miami to the Caribbean. You get on the cruise ship, and there are hundreds or thousands of other people on the ship. There are all these things you can do. The captain is steering the ship, but you get to choose what to do. You may play ping pong, you may watch someone play shuffleboard, you may go swimming, you may do all kinds of things. You can go eat, and you can choose from all kinds of places to eat. Guess what—the ship is still going on its course. The captain is steering it. God is in control. God has a plan. We're on the boat, and we're making choices, but we're not in control.

There was a medical missionary named Helen Revere who had done nothing but help people. Then war broke out, and the Revolutionaries took her captive. They humiliated her and repeatedly raped her. She was a doctor, so they physically did harm to her hands so she could no longer do her work.

She was eventually released and went back to Britain to recover. As she was recovering, she had to deal with all the pain and questions. Eventually she wrote out this question, as if God was asking her: "Can you thank Me for trusting you (Helen) with the experience, even if I never tell you why?" She'd been humiliated and mutilated and beaten, yet she imagined God was asking, "Hey Helen, can you trust Me to trust you with this situation even if I never tell you why?"

Two questions: Can you thank God? Can you thank Him, and can you trust Him for that hard time in your life? One more question. Can you trust the truth and not your feelings?

Let's get down to the bottom line. We serve a God Who is in control, Who is bigger than our situation, Who is bigger than we are. We serve a God Who created all things—darkness, peace, and calamity. Ultimately, we have to say, "Yes, I trust You. I trust Your Word. I trust You." When you come to the matter of salvation, you can't advance, you can't go forward, you can't move until you've come to that point where you can say, "I trust You," understanding that He does things differently than we would.

In Isaiah again, shortly after where it talks about God creating all these things, Isaiah writes this in 55:8–9, with God speaking: "For My thoughts are not your thoughts, Nor are your ways My ways, says the LORD. For as the heavens are higher than the earth, So are My ways higher than your ways, And My thoughts than your thoughts."

I can't think the thoughts that God thinks. I have my little brain, and I think a certain way. But God says, "Your thoughts are not my thoughts, and your ways are not my ways." Sometimes we just don't get it. So what we do is we begin to make up our own myths, our own misconceptions, instead of dealing with the truth and saying, "I believe You."

But it doesn't have to be that way. We have the choice right now. Will you choose to believe Him?

chapter 3

Christianity does not Own Truth
Michael Laymon

When you hear someone teaching that Christianity is the true, right way, what do you think? Have you ever wondered if, on the other side of the world, a Buddhist teacher could be telling his student the same thing? Or in the Middle East, that a Muslim is learning that Islam is the only way to Heaven?

What about the person next to you at school? Do you have any friends who don't think there is a God but say they are pretty sure of what is true? How about people with religions similar to Christianity—which of the parts that are different are true?

Many facts have been proven, and most people have experienced things in their lives that they say are true for sure. But beyond science and personal experience and religious traditions, how can we really know what is true? What is truth?

What can we know is always right at all times for all people in all places? What can we hold onto?

That's what we want to look at in this chapter.

Opinions and views are all around you in everyday life, and whether you realize it, they are all trying to convince you that they are true. So, before we tackle the big question of what truth is, let's start by looking at some systems of thought we deal with in today's culture. By first separating out these different views, we can see whether they work and which parts of these ideas may be pointing to real truth.

1. Secular Humanism: The belief that humanity is the highest of all beings. Truth and knowledge rest in science and human reason. This system emphasizes belief that there is no God; rather, we can look to ourselves to find meaning, purpose, and truth.

2. Cosmic Humanism: The New Age movement is based in mysticism and sees the world as "all is one." It has a common vision of a coming "new age" of peace and mass enlightenment. In this view, everything is part of one being and the same essence or reality. All that is, is god. Man, a part of "all that is," is also divine.

3. Marxism: The ideology of Karl Marx, based on atheism, materialism, evolution, and socialism. Marx's social system, communism, has the dream of a future utopia where all resources are owned by everyone in a society without classes. Marx said communism could be achieved by revolution of the masses in his 1848 book *The Communist Manifesto.*

4. Islam: This belief system, which has many similarities to Christianity, is different in that it denies that Jesus is God. In this view, Jesus was a great prophet, but not the Son of God, and the Trinity does not exist. As part of this, Jesus' death and resurrection—and thus all the teachings of salvation and New Testament sanctification—are also considered untrue. The Muslim holy book, the Koran, is considered the only true book (not the Bible, which is not trusted), and people are judged according to their good and bad works.

5. Postmodernism: A philosophical idea that reality is ultimately inaccessible by human investigation, that knowledge is a social construction, that truth claims are political power plays, and that the meaning of words is to be determined by readers, not authors.

Basically, reality is what individuals or social groups make it to be. This worldview can be seen in modern society when people say that truth can't be known, that everyone should do what's best for them, and that we should be tolerant and accepting of everyone's views.

6. Christianity

What makes this discussion even more difficult is that a lot of these worldviews overlap. For example, Christians are called to be kind and understanding. This sometimes means being tolerant of other people's views while they are slowly brought to the point where the Holy Spirit shows them the truth. But Christians would never support outright tolerance of all views, and letting people just do whatever. So, which of these ideas is true? Tolerance or non-tolerance? Where is the balance? At what point should Christians do one and not the other? Where is the *standard* for truth—the one thing we can keep coming back to that doesn't change with time or circumstances?

These are essential questions, because by answering them, we're figuring out whether Christianity is the right way. If you look at all these worldviews, parts of each of them look good. They were all developed by people with good intentions. But Christianity shouldn't be followed because it looks the best. We shouldn't believe it because of its historical proof, or all the good things people have done in its name. We have to have a better reason.

Do you ever wonder whether Christianity is right? If not, why not? What makes you so sure you are right? Think about what has given you questions. Maybe you've seen people in other religions who are really sincere about their faith. Maybe they have certain beliefs that just make a lot more sense. Maybe some parts of Christianity seem to contradict themselves—or maybe Christianity as a whole just doesn't make sense to you. It's not logical, or it seems to cause more problems than it solves.

These are all valid concerns, and they are areas we should be exploring. We don't want to believe something just to believe it, or because someone told us it was true once. This isn't a "good bet"— that Christianity has more stuff going for it than other religions.

No way—Christianity has everything going for it, and it's our job to personally make sure we understand why.

Millions of people believe these other religions. Many people think that any of these worldviews work—that they all lead to the same place. But God has promised us in the Bible that if we look for truth, He will show it to us. It takes some effort, but we can know. Our belief can be based on something solid.

So, let's look at the main question of this chapter: Do Christians own the truth? The answer—believe it or not—is no. Christianity, and everything we associate with it—certain people, certain behaviors, certain stories—does not own the truth. God owns the truth, and we need to hold Christianity up to what He says is true.

Do you get what I'm saying? There's a difference between God and Christianity. Christianity encapsulates what God has communicated to us, but it's not truth in itself. It just communicates truth. Christianity is true because it reflects Who God is and what God says, not because this particular belief system, or the people who live it, are true.

By understanding this, we take away a huge part of the questions and misconceptions people have against Christianity. *Look at all the evil that's been done in the name of Christianity. Look how many Christians are hypocrites. Look at the different traditions. Look at the bickering in churches. Look at how Christians' arguments don't make sense. Look at how many followers of Christianity aren't sincere.* These are all criticisms of a system—what Christians have done with the truth God has given us—rather than criticisms of truth.

The truth can't be argued with. It's unchanging and affects people. It convicts them. That's what the word "truth" means—that it's inarguably right. So, as we're trying to get to the bottom of what truth is, maybe it's best not to focus on whether Christianity owns the truth. Let's look instead at the question, "What is truth?" And now that we know truth is God, let's ask, "Who is God?" The answer to this will help us see how God communicates through Christianity. Then we can know why we can believe Christianity, support it, and share it with people of other religions. We can show them the source of truth: God.

So, Who is God? Well, if you think you're getting that answer here, you're going to be disappointed—no one has ever answered that question completely! But as we learned in chapter [Christians are stupid], God *can* be known. We can understand parts of Him and learn more. So, let's start with where we can see God—how God has revealed Himself in this world we see each day. This is where we find truth.

God has revealed Himself to us in three main ways: through creation—the world we live in, through Scripture, and through Jesus Christ.

The first way, **through creation,** is the most obvious way we can see God. So obvious, in fact, that it's easy to think this is just the way the world is, and not look for God in it. The Bible has some great examples of God reaching people through nature. Think of Psalms especially and how David and other writers saw God in the world around them (Psalm 19:1).

But what about you? Where do you see God in nature?

How about science class? Do you ever think about the Creator's role in the complex and beautiful world around us?

So many of God's attributes (characteristics that describe Who He is) are evident in the world we live in. The order and logic of the universe reflect God. The aesthetics of landscapes or changing weather point back to His quest to make things beautiful. Life itself—growth, strength, personality—all these characteristics reflected the God Who made them. Many of the things we are most sure about around us are rooted in how God has created the world and shows Himself in it.

So, what does nature tell us about truth? If God is revealed in the world around us, what should we be doing with it? Some of the worldviews we looked at earlier are based on the idea that nature itself is a god—and we're part of nature. By taking care of the world and seeing where we fit in, they say, we can find meaning. But God teaches us that nature isn't it. The world is a path to, a reflection of, how He reveals Himself. We use what we see of Him in nature to learn about Him and pursue Him. Nature is just the first step.

Romans 1:20 gives us a good explanation of how helpful the world around us can be in knowing God. It says, "For since the creation of the world His invisible *attributes* are clearly seen, being understood by the things that are made, *even* His eternal power and Godhead, so that they are without excuse." Paul says "no excuse." What we see around us is enough for us to look for God, no excuses! We have been made with the ability to sense, see, and understand God—and truth—from nature.

But God didn't stop there. He also gave us **Scripture to help us further find truth.** Many different applications can be drawn from the world around us, so God gave us a distinct set of stories, instructions, and principles to guide us in our search for Him and truth.

The Bible has all kinds of different teaching in it, all hand-picked by God (2 Peter 1:20–21). In the Old Testament, we get accounts of how the world was created and how God set up the nation of Israel. God guided different sets of people with different instructions, from the one tree Adam and Eve could eat from in the Garden of Eden, to His instruction to Abraham to trust Him as He guided his steps, to His establishment of the nation of Israel with its many laws and commandments. Scripture gives us specific applications of God's truth for people dealing with different situations all throughout history.

If you're familiar with the Bible, you have noticed that it leaves a lot of questions unanswered. That's because Scripture is not supposed to be a comprehensive account of history, or a complete rulebook. The point is not to record every detail of human life, or to have a "do this" for every possible problem. **The point of the Bible is to see Who God is and how He communicates His truth to mankind.** God has picked which parts of history and what guidelines we get to see. One thing we can know for sure, though, is that what He has given us will lead us to truth. In 2 Timothy 3:16–17 it says, "All Scripture is given by inspiration of God, and is profitable for doctrine, for reproof, for correction, for instruction in righteousness, that the man of God may be complete, thoroughly equipped for every good work."

The final way we see truth, and the most important way, is **through Jesus Christ.** This is where the real differences come in. Other religions say you can see truth in nature, but it's then interpreted by each of us. Other religions go to the next step and have holy books. They say the rules and instructions tell us how to live. But these are also written by men, and they are being used by people like us, who, even with all these bits of truth in front of us, still can't get to the bottom of it by ourselves. **The difference with Christianity is in its name: Jesus Christ is the living bridge between God and man. Through Him, we can see truth in life and know it for ourselves.**

There are several distinguishing factors that make Jesus unique. First, He was definitely human. Unlike other beliefs, the Bible teaches that Christianity's Savior was here in a body, experiencing life just like us.

Second, He was God (Matthew 16:15–17; John 10:24–33; John 20:28–29). You know that's why Jesus was killed, right? Because He claimed to be God. Plenty of people have called themselves great prophets, shared legitimate truth, and done miracles. But they didn't call themselves God. Jesus did—repeatedly—and proved it with His miracles and His understanding of truth.

You see, mankind had truth in the world and in Scripture, but until it had Someone Who could totally understand people (humans) and totally understand God (the Son of God), there was no way to make the connection complete.

The third thing that sets Jesus, and Christianity, apart from other religions is that Jesus presented Himself as the way to take care of our eternal destination. Other religions emphasize *doing* something— either changing something about us to become better in touch with our nature, or doing something (such as good works) to follow the rule books and earn favor with God. Jesus went beyond that and said it is not our efforts that will save us. He alone can provide a guaranteed path to Heaven.

In John 14:6, Jesus told His disciples, "I am the way, the truth, and the life. No one comes to the Father except through Me." That's it— He's the only way! Other belief systems look like they get close, but He is the only guaranteed way.

We know how this plays out in the Bible. Jesus, being both God and man, died a physical death to take away our spiritual death and sin. When He rose again, that gave us a chance at new life, too. By believing in Who He is and what He has done—by trusting in Him to close the gap—we can be saved.

But what about these other religions? Why does Jesus have to be the *only* way?

Let's review the reasons why Jesus is different from other religions. First, He was a man. Other religions often have a god looking down on people. If he's any real kind of god, he can't reach out to those people because they are flawed mortals. So, they are required to work their way toward him. But does this work? Can we ever do enough good? Don't we still do wrong? And is this kind of god—a judge that weighs good and bad and accepts only some people—is this kind of god reflected in the world around us? Is this god the source of this life's order, beauty, and personality? Jesus solved the problem by experiencing life as we do. He came to us since we could never work our way to Him. He also provided a payment for our sinfulness that we couldn't pay, and He didn't do it by lowering His standards. His humanity took the payment while He was still a totally righteous, just God.

Second, Jesus was still God. He wasn't just a great human doing cool tricks. Religions all over the world have plenty of those guys—good teachers, good prophets. But those people are limited. They don't have a full understanding of the truth because they are not God. Worse yet, they can't promise new life—because they're all dead! Confucius, Buddha, Mohammed—the list goes on. They part of the truth, but not the truth that could bring lasting life. It only gave a hint of what that life could be. Without Christ, and the change that belief in Him brings, even the greatest earthly wisdom will fall short.

The final way Jesus is different, that He secured our eternal destination, is the most important. Look at these other religions. Many are surprisingly low on guarantees that they'll be right in the end. "Hope you do enough good works!" they say. "Hope you find nirvana!" Jesus doesn't ask us to hope for that. He tells us to trust Him. "I've got it taken care of," He says. "No work required on your part."

Now, it's great that we've just seen why Christianity is it—why it's different from other religions and why it has the truth. But that doesn't mean we've answered all the questions.

What about all these other religions? Are they all wrong? Like we said before, many religions have parts that line up with the truth God has shown us. Take pantheism, for example. In this belief, God is in everything, and our goal is to understand nature and see how we're a part of it. These basic ideas are close with Christianity—yes, we can see God reflected in the world, and we can use it to understand Him. But a bush won't save us; Jesus will. And unless someone believing another religion has Jesus, they are missing a fundamental part. These other religions may be helpful in pointing people to an understanding of God, but until they have Jesus, the journey is not complete.

But what about your unsaved friends? They are so sincere about what they believe. And what about all those Christians who are hypocrites? What about people who call themselves followers of Jesus but don't live like Him? Are we really saying that the sincere people are wrong, that the hypocrites are right, that Jesus is the only Way, Truth, and Life?

The sad answer here is people's actions can't define the truth. Truth is not controlled by hypocrisy or sincerity. Truth is always truth, no matter who is trying to use it.

Let's look at a baseball fan as an example. A person can get himself really worked up that the Pittsburgh Pirates are going to win the World Series. But if the Pirates don't have any good batters and anyone who can throw 90 feet, is that belief going to mean anything? That team will not only lose a lot, but maybe those players shouldn't even be on the field! Belief has to be based on something that will work.

In the same way, a lot of people can believe in the right thing without knowing all of what they're trusting in. Let's go back to baseball. Have you ever seen someone wearing a New York Yankees jersey who didn't know who any of the players were? That's how a lot of Christians are. They found the right thing—Jesus—but don't know much about Him other than He saved them. Unfortunately, hypocrites will always be around, but that can't keep us from looking for the truth. It is still true, even if they abuse it. We can't let our foundation be moved by people not living correctly.

Remember, too, that when we talk about truth, we are talking about Who God is and what He says that means. What we've covered in this chapter—Who Jesus is and why He is the answer—is the truth we are interested in. Christianity has gathered a lot of add-ons over the years. Rules and traditions tell us what clothes to wear, what words to use, when to go to church, what music to listen to, and on and on. Now, these things are helpful for pointing us *toward* the truth and giving us practical guidelines for Biblical principles. But we can't confuse them for Christianity. *Jesus* is the Way, the Truth, and the Life. He is what we should be pointing people to. The rest is just extra help.

So, where does this leave us with our questions about truth?

There is something we all need to understand. Truth is not relative to our situations or formed from our own opinions. It's already there, and we're all just coming at it from different points.

1. Truth is objective—it is something we discover. God embodies what truth is and shows it to us through nature, Scripture, and Jesus. Truth is not subject to whether we like it or choose to use it. It's always there.

2. Truth is consistent—it does not change according to our situations or circumstances.

3. Truth is relevant—Christians may not own the truth, but they know it. Many people don't. Christians' responsibility is to share what they know about God and His truth with people who haven't heard or have an incomplete idea of truth.

Pieces of truth are in the world all around us. They are in religion, history, science, and philosophy, and especially throughout our personal experiences. Our job is to help people along the path of truth until they find the One Who wraps it all together.

We have to understand, though, that not all people want complete truth. We like the idea of truth, but deep down we want it because of what it will get for us. We want to know what's true so we can use it.

We want to be in control of what we do and understand.

In 2 Timothy 4:3–4 it says, "For the time will come when they will not endure sound doctrine, but according to their own desires, because they have itching ears, they will heap up for themselves teachers; and they will turn their ears away from the truth, and be turned aside to fables." These verses are saying that people look for truth that lines up with what they already believe. They want to make it relative to their life situations.

Proverbs 1:28–29 speaks of the person who rejects the ultimate truth: "Then they will call on me, but I will not answer. They will seek me diligently, but they will not find me, because they hated knowledge and did not choose the fear of the LORD." This is describing people who try to come to God too late, when they have already rejected the truth He was trying to give them.

That's why it's so important to get this truth to people. Some may reject it, but others just need to hear. Think about things that have been hurdles toward you hearing or accepting the truth before. Were hypocritical or insincere Christians harmful to you in your pursuit of truth? How can you aim to not be that way to others, to better clear the way for them to hear God's truth? Take some time today to think about how you will share truth to those around you.

Before that, though, look inside. Can you say with certainty that you know the Truth? What are you going to do about it?

Your Heaven is My Hell
Kris Stout

A lot of us have questions about what Heaven is really like.

For some of us, it doesn't seem like a big deal—sitting on a cloud, playing a harp forever. Doing the same thing over and over again—it doesn't seem like a lot of fun. It seems pretty boring, actually.

Maybe you're not excited about the idea of Heaven because you can think of something or someone that won't be there. Maybe it's a friend or a pet that you know won't be in Heaven.

Or what about all your favorite things—will they be in Heaven? You hear people talk about "Heaven on earth," and you can imagine what that means for you. Maybe it's ESPN on a 60-inch HD flatscreen, nonstop games, and unlimited amounts of food. Maybe it's a never-ending shopping trip. Or having an endless supply of chocolate that doesn't make you fat. You know what your favorite things are, and maybe your view of Heaven is having those things or doing those things, nonstop.

Some people think Heaven is like karma, where what you do to other people comes back to you.

Maybe you've never thought about Heaven; it probably seems a long way off. Why should you have to worry about it now?

My 16-year-old cousin finished mowing the lawn one day, went in, laid down, and told his mom he wasn't feeling good. The next morning my aunt came in to wake him up, and he was gone. He had a heart murmur. We never think about those kinds of things. You may think, "Heaven, that's far away. It doesn't concern me. I've never thought about what Heaven may be like."

But whether it's something right around the corner, understanding Heaven is a big part of the Christian faith. For some people, not understanding Heaven keeps them from accepting Christianity. For others, not having this part of the Christian experience tacked down in their heads can change the way they approach their relationship with God.

When people don't want to go to Heaven, it's because they are missing something. Most of what we think about Heaven is from some preconception that we've gotten from television, culture or some other source. We don't really have a clear idea of what the truth about Heaven really is. Maybe we think about how our grandparents described it to us. Maybe we think about it as something we read in a Hallmark card.

If we really knew the truth and understood what God says about Heaven then there would be no place we would rather be.

1 Corinthians 2:9 says, "Eye has not seen, nor ear heard, Nor have entered into the heart of man the things which God has prepared for those who love Him." Do you understand that verse? Take a moment and let that sink in. What God is saying is that the wildest imaginings you could come up with, the most fabulous and most unbelievable place you can think of, those ideas in your head don't even start to explain this incredible place called Heaven. We cannot even imagine all that God has prepared for those who love Him.

The only One with a clear idea of what Heaven is really like is God, so let's take a look at what He's told us. Remember, no matter how great Heaven seems even now as we look at scripture, it is even greater than that!

In John 14:2, Jesus said, "In My Father's house are many mansions; if it were not so, I would have told you. I go to prepare a place for you." **The first thing that God tells us is that Heaven is a welcoming place.** What does that mean? He says, "In My Father's house are many mansions." Jesus describes Heaven as a home. It's not just a place that's somewhere out there; it's a home for you and me. It's a welcoming place. Heaven will not be a distant, cold place. Heaven is a home. Not just any home, it's **your** home! It says, "In My Father's house." If you know Jesus Christ as your personal Savior, you're a son or daughter of the Son of God. He is your Father, and just like earthly fathers provide shelter for their children, so does God. It's your house. A perfect Father, a perfect home—it's a welcoming place.

In the same verse it says, "I go to prepare a place for you." It's not just a welcoming place; **it's a prepared place.** It's not some great expanse of nothingness, or a place you move into that needs some work. God is preparing this amazing home for you and for me right now. He's preparing it!

Someone once said, "It took God seven days to create the universe, but He's been working on Heaven for 2,000 years." That's pretty amazing.

Next, it's not just a prepared place; **it's a personal place.** What does that mean? He says, "I go to prepare a place *for you.*" It's not like some impersonal amusement park where you'll be lost in the crowd. I'm from Ohio, with the greatest amusement park on the face of this earth: Cedar Point. You walk into Cedar Point, and you have to pay an outrageous fee to get in. You're there with tens of thousands of people, and it's fabulous—but they don't care about you. Heaven isn't like that. It's personal. Think of it as an amusement park made especially for you—your favorite rides, your favorite kinds of food, your favorite colors. It's the same idea; the perfect God Who knows you has a personal Heaven for you.

It is also a happy and satisfying place. In Revelation 7:16–17, we read this: "They shall neither hunger anymore nor thirst anymore; the sun shall not strike them, nor any heat; for the Lamb who is in the midst of the throne will shepherd them and lead them to living fountains of waters. And God will wipe away every tear from their eyes." Heaven will be a happy and satisfying place. What does that mean? Look at the verse—no hunger. That doesn't necessarily mean that we're not going to eat—the Bible mentions the marriage supper of the Lamb. What it's saying is that you're not going to have the physical limitations of hunger. On earth, so much of our life is centered on eating. We get a job to feed ourselves, because otherwise we won't live! So much of the pain and death in the world is from people not having enough food. But this is not the case in Heaven.

You know what, in Heaven, you probably aren't going to gain weight. I could deal with that! That would be Heaven in itself for me—all I can eat and I don't have to worry about if my pants are going to fit tomorrow.

Not only will there be no hunger, but there will be no famine or poverty, no thirst, the perfect climate and temperature. These verses say the sun will not scorch; cold will not freeze. It will be perfect.

There will also be fullness of life in every way. No sorrow or tears. God said He will lead us to the rivers and springs of life. These are not just images; these are realities. That's exciting!

As we look at all of this, we start saying, "Wow, that's pretty amazing!" And remember, it has not even entered into your heart or your mind how incredible it is.

No sorrow or tears. How many of our lives have been spent in sorrow or feeling torn apart? Are you hurting right now because of something that has happened to you? There will be no more of that. God promises you that as you enter Heaven, there will be no more sorrow, no more tears. Not only will our heavenly home be way better than anything on this earth, personalized for us, but it will also be free of all the terrible parts of this earth.

Best yet, in Heaven we will be in God's presence. He's the One that makes all this happen—the One Who gave His life for you. It says He will wipe every tear from your eyes, and there will be no more sorrow and no more pain. It's a happy and satisfying place.

Hebrews 11:16 says **it is a better place.** "But now they desire a better, that is, a heavenly country. Therefore God is not ashamed to be called their God, for He has prepared a city for them." A better place. I mentioned people saying they have Heaven on earth, but that's way off! It is so much better than Heaven on earth. Take the greatest experience that you could ever imagine here on this planet, the greatest thing, the most awesome time you could ever experience with your friends, the most fabulous time that you could ever have on vacation, the most fulfilled, the most excited, the most amazing—take all of that, and God says, "I got something better for you."

Part of the reason it's a better place is because **it is a new place.** Revelation 21 talks about Heaven: "Now I saw a new Heaven and a new earth, for the first Heaven and the first earth had passed away. ... There shall be no more pain, for the former things have passed away.' Then He who sat on the throne said, 'Behold, I make all things new.'"

Everything is made new. Heaven is a new place. What does that mean? The old Heaven and the old earth are gone. You see, Heaven isn't some place in the sky. It is a real, tangible place that God is going to make. He takes our fallen world and makes a new Heaven and new earth. From all we can tell in Scripture, we are going to be able to enjoy both for all eternity—a new planet, forever new, forever young, forever perfect, and a new Heaven that we will be able to know and explore and enjoy.

You know the best part of the new Heaven and new earth? It will have new life. Your life, which passed from death to life if you've accepted Christ as your Savior, will be changed into a new, perfect life. The work started on the cross, and all the growth in your relationship with God becomes new life in this new Heaven and earth. It's the end of your life, everything you regret, everything that isn't true. Some people say they finish their life without any regrets, but you know what? I think that somebody who finishes their life without regrets is probably someone who has not looked close enough. We all have regrets. But you know what's so amazing about Heaven? God says He makes all things new. All the things from the first life are passed away. That's one of the reasons He can wipe all the tears away from our eyes, because He looks at your life, and He looks at your whole experience, and He says, "In Heaven, all things are made new."

Heaven is also a beautiful place. Check out Revelation 21:10–22:2:

> "...and showed me the great city, the holy Jerusalem, descending out of heaven from God, having the glory of God. Her light was like a most precious stone, like a jasper stone, clear as crystal. Also she had a great and high wall with twelve gates, and twelve angels at the gates, and names written on them, which are the names of the twelve tribes of the children of Israel: three gates on the east, three gates on the north, three gates on the south, and three gates on the west. Now the wall of the city had twelve foundations, and on them were the names of the twelve apostles of the Lamb. And he who talked with me had a gold reed to measure the city, its gates, and its wall. The city is laid out as a square; its length is as great as its breadth. And he measured the city with the reed: twelve thousand furlongs. Its length, breadth, and height are equal. Then he measured its wall: one hundred and forty-four cubits, according to the measure of a man, that is, of an angel. The construction of its wall was of jasper; and the city was pure gold, like clear glass. The foundations of the wall of the city were adorned with all kinds of precious stones: the first foundation was jasper, the second sapphire, the third chalcedony, the fourth emerald, the fifth sardonyx, the sixth sardius, the seventh chrysolite, the eighth beryl, the ninth topaz, the tenth chrysoprase, the eleventh jacinth, and the twelfth amethyst. The twelve gates were twelve pearls: each individual gate was of one pearl. And the street of the city was pure gold, like transparent glass. But I saw no temple in it, for the Lord God Almighty and the Lamb are its temple. The city had no need of the sun or of the moon to shine in it, for the glory of God

illuminated it. The Lamb is its light. And the nations of those who are saved shall walk in its light, and the kings of the earth bring their glory and honor into it. Its gates shall not be shut at all by day (there shall be no night there). And they shall bring the glory and the honor of the nations into it. But there shall by no means enter it anything that defiles, or causes an abomination or a lie, but only those who are written in the Lamb's Book of Life. And he showed me a pure river of water of life, clear as crystal, proceeding from the throne of God and of the Lamb. In the middle of its street, and on either side of the river, was the tree of life, which bore twelve fruits, each tree yielding its fruit every month. The leaves of the tree were for the healing of the nations."

Enough said. Heaven is a beautiful place.

And remember, all we just read—what God has prepared for you will blow all that away.

Finally, do you remember the idea of us hanging out on a cloud, playing a harp and staying there forever and ever? That seems pretty boring. If that's true, we won't be doing anything. That idea isn't correct; Heaven is a busy place. We will not be just hanging out playing a harp, but we will be an active society in Heaven serving God and reigning with Him forever and ever.

Your first thought may be that service doesn't sound like fun. (I knew you were thinking this so follow my thought here) Did you know that the concept of work was found in the Bible before the curse and the fall of man? Adam was in the Garden of Eden with Eve, and they were given the job of taking care of the garden. When they did that, they had to name all the animals, etc., and then the Fall happened. When God came and talked to them about the consequences of their sin, He said that work would then be a curse—it wouldn't be fun. Something that was supposed to be good for Adam and Eve became difficult and a punishment because of their sin. But in Heaven, we're going to be able to enjoy work like it's meant to be. It will be a good thing.

From what we see here in Revelation, there are nations and kings, and we are serving God. You know what else we will be doing? We will be reigning with Him. We will have dominion over the earth, and we will enjoy it. We will never tire, we will never thirst, we will never hunger, and we will be busy serving God. One of the things that makes this a difficult concept is that we are so indoctrinated to this world and our own society. It is hard for us to grasp the truth of how now only our bodies will be transformed but so will our minds. I assure you that you will have a new value system. So we have the myth that Heaven is some feathery, non-descript place that may or may not exist. We also have the misconception that as long as you're good outweighs your bad, you should make it in OK. The idea for most people is, "Hey, if Heaven exists, I deserve it. If I'm good enough, I deserve to go to Heaven, whatever it is."

You may think that as you're reading this. But I have to tell you the truth, that is just a misconception that many people hold today. It's not true. There is nothing in God's Word that suggests Heaven is just some nice place where people hang out after they die. The Bible does not say that being a good person will guarantee your future in Heaven.

What is the truth? It's what we see in scripture, that you need to have a relationship with Jesus Christ. It starts at salvation, placing your trust in His death and resurrection. But it doesn't stop there. We know from scripture that God has a plan, and that everything happening on this earth is building toward what He wants for us. And remember John 14:2: "I go to prepare a place for you." In this chapter, we've seen that Heaven is a real place for *the children of God*. It's made specifically as a place of new life for those of us who have a relationship with God.

So my question for you right now is this: "Jesus has prepared a place for you, but are you prepared for it?" God is working on Heaven. He says that He's preparing it. Heaven will be ready for you, and it's wonderful beyond your wildest imagination. But are you ready for Heaven? You may ask, "What do you mean, Ready for Heaven? How can I get ready for Heaven?"

It's real simple. Revelation 21:27 says "only those who are written in the Lamb's Book of Life" will go to Heaven. It says, "But there shall by no means enter it anything that defiles, or causes an abomination or a lie, but only those who are written in the Lamb's Book of Life." Heaven has nothing to do with whether you deserve it, because the Gospel has shown us that the only way to be good enough is through Jesus Christ.

When you believe on Jesus Christ and His way of salvation, He will write your name in the Lamb's Book of Life. There are a lot of misconceptions about Heaven, but the Bible tells us it is a real place for people who have real relationships with God. This is good news. But it also means you have a decision to make: Do you want this Heaven? Do you know the God Who is preparing places for His children in this Heaven? What are you going to do about the truth today?

Your Hell is my Heaven
Kris Stout

We spent the last chapter talking about Heaven and how people have misconceptions of what Heaven really is. A lot of ideas have crept into our culture of what we think Heaven is, or what we want it to be.

In this chapter, we're going to talk about another place about which there are just as many misconceptions: Hell. Just the word is probably enough to bring a bunch of different ideas to your head.

Similar to the way people associate good things on earth with Heaven, a lot of times people think something they've experienced on earth is like Hell. For instance, when someone has a day (or longer!) when things really don't go their way, or when they're dealing with the consequences of sin, we'll hear people say they're experiencing "Hell on earth."

Other people use Hell to represent all the bad things they like to do. When I lived in France, there was this event called "Hellfest," where all these people showed up to celebrate Hell. There was heavy metal music, and they treated Hell like it was fun—partying, no rules, no limits. There was endless drugs, beer, sex. It was like total anarchy.

A lot of people act like Hell would be fun because of who will be there. You know, Heaven is for all the goody-goodys, so the cool people will be in Hell. Other people don't like the idea of a judging God, so they say they'd rather be in Hell. I've heard a lot of people say they want to be in Hell because that's where all their friends will be. They can do anything they want there.

These are common ideas we have about Hell—what Hell has become in our culture. Hell can't be that bad.

I found something interesting, though. A recent survey found that 74% of people believe in Heaven, but only 59 percent believe in Hell. You know why? Because Hell is not a very nice place. It's easier for people to act like it doesn't exist because deep down, I think most people know it's not as nice as they like to think it is. The reality of a place like Hell existing is very, very scary to people.

We don't like to be around things that make us uncomfortable; we don't even like to hear about them. Think about the disasters and tragedies around the world. Think about that huge earthquake in Haiti, and all those people crying and suffering. Seeing those images is hard for us. And so much of what we see in the media is already cleaned up because the nature of these horrifying events is just so unsettling.

So, what do we do? When we see people hurting in Haiti or hear about a great tragedy, or even if we see something like an animal suffering, what do we do? We turn it off. We go away. We look somewhere else. It makes us uncomfortable, so we don't think about it.

That's the way a lot of people feel about Hell. Many people who call themselves Christians, and even some great churches today, don't want to talk about a literal place called Hell because it sounds so unpleasant. But just like those people in Haiti are suffering whether our TV is on or not, Hell is still real whether we acknowledge it or not.

Just as the Bible speaks of the wonders of Heaven, it also speaks clearly and often about the reality of Hell. Jesus Himself talked about it, too. In Matthew 10:28, Jesus said, "And do not fear those who kill the body but cannot kill the soul. But rather fear Him who is able to destroy both soul and body in Hell." The word that Jesus uses is actually the word *gana*, which was a place on the south side of Jerusalem where trash and dead bodies of animals and criminals were burned. It was an image for the people of eternal punishment, the fire of Hell. It burned continually, and it didn't just burn, it stunk. It was a place that was disgusting. It was repulsive, and no one wanted to be near it.

In Luke 16, Jesus tells the story of the rich man and Lazarus. He does this to teach us some of the realities of Hell. Look at what verses 19–31 say:

> " There was a certain rich man who was clothed in purple and fine linen and fared sumptuously every day. But there was a certain beggar named Lazarus, full of sores, who was laid at his gate, desiring to be fed with the crumbs which fell from the rich man's table. Moreover the dogs came and licked his sores. So it was that the beggar died, and was carried by the angels to Abraham's bosom. The rich man also died and was buried. And being in torments in Hades, he lifted up his eyes and saw Abraham afar off, and Lazarus in his bosom. "Then he cried and said, 'Father Abraham, have mercy on me, and send Lazarus that he may dip the tip of his finger in water and cool my tongue; for I am tormented in this flame.' But Abraham said, 'Son, remember that in your lifetime you received your good things, and likewise Lazarus evil things; but now he is comforted and you are tormented. And besides all this, between us and you there is a great gulf fixed, so that those who want to pass from here to you cannot, nor can those from there pass to us.' "Then he said, 'I beg you therefore, father, that you would send him to my father's house, for I have five brothers, that he may testify to them, lest they also come to this place of torment.' Abraham said to him, 'They have Moses and the prophets; let them hear them.' And he said, 'No, father Abraham; but if one goes to them from the dead, they will repent.' But he said to him, 'If they do not hear Moses and the prophets, neither will they be persuaded though one rise from the dead.'"

What are some things we should notice about Hell? See that it says nothing about a devil with horns, a pitchfork, and a tail—that's not in the Bible.

First of all, people are conscious in Hell. This rich man is engaged in active, conscious thought and conversation. In verse 23, "He lifted up his eyes being in torment." In verse 24 he cried out and said something. In verse 25 he could hear as Abraham spoke to him.

People are not only conscious; these verses say they are also tormented. **People are tormented in Hell.** It seems kind of obvious, but listen to what it says. Some people today think that Hell is a place where you are annihilated, where you don't feel anything, and where you just fade out of existence. This man was in torment, in agony. He was begging for someone. He was so desperate that he was begging for someone to just dip the tip of his finger in water and give him a little bit of refreshment on his tongue. He was in that much agony. The flames are real.

In verse 28, notice that he's fully aware. **People can remember in Hell.** The rich man remembered his former life. He remembered his five brothers and his home. Think about that. One of the glories of Heaven is the fact that Jesus Christ will wipe every tear away from our eyes and that all the things that were before will pass away. We will no longer remember the sorrows and the suffering of this life. But one of the greatest tortures and agonies of Hell is that you will remember forever and ever and ever with regret. You will remember when you had an opportunity to do something about it. You'll remember the good deeds and the bad. You'll remember. You'll remember not trusting God for salvation.

In verse 26 we are told that "none may cross over between Hell and Heaven." Quite simply, **people cannot escape from Hell.** Many people think God is going to give them a second chance. They think, "God is a God of grace and mercy and love, so if I get there and realize how awful it is, I'll say, 'Excuse me, God, I think I made a mistake. Could I have a do-over? Could I maybe just get out of here? It's getting a little hot.'" No. Jesus said there is a great chasm fixed between Hell and Heaven and that none can cross over. People cannot escape from Hell.

As bad as it is, in verses 27–28 we see that **people in Hell do not want others to go there.** This blows away the idea that all our friends are there, so we want to go and be with them. People in Hell would never wish their fate on anyone else—it's that bad. Anyone there, if given the chance, would warn people so they too would not end up in that place of torment.

The hard part about this is what Abraham tells the rich man—those in Hell cannot use the excuse that they didn't know. Everyone has been given ample warning—God's Word is available, and the truth is out there. They were not in Hell because they didn't know how bad it is—but because they rejected God and His truth. If they would not listen to God, they would not listen even if a man raised from the dead comes and tells them. They made their decision.

Those are some of the realities of Hell. Such an awful place may lead us to ask why Hell even exists. Why would God create such a terrible place? We know that Hell is real, and now we need to look at the reason it exists. In Matthew 25:40, Jesus said, speaking of Himself, "The King will answer and say to them, 'And the King will answer and say to them, 'Assuredly, I say to you, inasmuch as you did it to one of the least of these My brethren, you did it to Me.' Then He will also say to those on His left, 'Depart from Me, accursed ones, into the eternal fire which has been prepared for the devil and his angels.'" Jesus is saying that Hell was not prepared for you and me, or any other person. He didn't set it up from the beginning to punish people who got on His bad side. Hell was made for the devil and his angels. In fact, we're reminded in 2 Peter 3:9, "The Lord is not slack concerning His promise, as some count slackness, but is longsuffering toward us, not willing that any should perish but that all should come to repentance." That's what we believe. That is the greatest hope we have. God does not want you to perish. God does not want people to die, to be lost. He wants everyone to come to repentance, to come to that place where we were all originally intended to be. Hell wasn't made for you!

The problem is that although we started at the right place, with humanity having a relationship with a perfect and righteous God, our sin has created a problem. God is perfect, holy, and sinless, and so is His Heaven. Because God is perfectly sinless and holy and so is His Heaven, I **cannot spend eternity in His presence with my sin.** It's impossible. That's what Romans 3:23 means when it says, "For all have sinned and fall short of the glory of God." But there's another problem. Romans 6:23 says, "For the wages of sin is death."

There are three kinds of death we see in the Bible. Physical death is the separation of my body from my soul. Spiritual death, on the other hand, is the separation of my soul from God. This is what happened when we sinned. The "falling short," the "wages of sin," is a spiritual death where we are separated from God. Even though we are physically alive, we are spiritually dead.

The third death is eternal death. Eternal death is the separation of my body from my soul for all eternity. Sin is extremely offensive to God—it's against everything God stands for—and if we reject God through our sin while on this earth, not only can we not be in Heaven due to our sin, but we will also have eternal death. *Everyone* who has sinned is condemned to death.

You may say, "Wait a minute—we are all condemned to Hell?" We all have died spiritually, but on this earth we've been given a way out of eternal death. God has provided a way to patch up the gap that sin caused so we do not have to die eternally. The same verse that tells us that the wages of sin are death says that God gives eternal life through Jesus.

Some people will ask, "How can a loving God send people to Hell?" But the question should really be, "How can people choose Hell when there is a loving God?" Jesus, the perfect, eternal Son of God, came to earth and died so that you and I would not have to. He made a way for those of us who are condemned, who had no hope out of death and Hell, to leave that destiny and be reunited with God instead. We've already talked about the reality of Hell and the reason for Hell, but for me, the most amazing part of all of this is what I call the rescue from Hell. Why would Jesus do something like that for us? He left Heaven and died a horrible death. Why?

When God created us, we were created for Him—to have a relationship with Him. We were made for God, and that only stopped because of our sin. God loves us and wants that relationship again, and the only way that can happen is if our sin is taken care of. We need to be able to stand before a righteous God.

Romans 3:25 says, talking about Jesus, "Whom God set forth as a propitiation by His blood, through faith, to demonstrate His righteousness, because in His forbearance God had passed over the sins that were previously committed." What is propitiation? That means that while our sin—which is the opposite of God—offended Him, Christ's death made a way to pay for that sin. He took the punishment that had to be paid of our sinning and violating God's character. The physical punishment for sin is Hell and separation from God, but Christ paid for that.

Not only that—look further in the verse. It says He declared His righteousness. Not only are we saved from punishment, but Christ's death also means that we can now be in the presence of a righteous God in Heaven. You see, Hell isn't just about physical suffering. It's also about missing out on an essential part of us, what we were created for—being with God. In Hell, people are going to be separated from God forever.

Even today, whether you believe in God or not, God is still present. God is still working. That is a grace that many people do not understand. We live in the beauty of God's creation, and God reveals Himself to us in amazing ways. But when you are in Hell, you are completely separated from light and God for all eternity.

The same God of perfect holiness is also the God of perfect love. A common response to Hell is that it's terrible that anyone should have to go there. With that in mind, God finding a way to deliver us from that destination shows us just how loving He is. You may say, "What has God ever done for me? How has God ever proved to me that He loves me?"

Romans 5:8 says that God proved His love for us by dying for us. Not only did Jesus die, but He did it "while we were yet sinners"—while we were offending God with our wickedness, He extended love. Jesus even experienced that separation from God ("My God, my God, why hast Thou forsaken me?") when He died for us.

If you don't take away anything else from this chapter, get this. When Jesus Christ came 2,000 years ago and hung on that cross, He did it for you. He did it because He loves you, and He does not want you to spend an eternity in Hell. He doesn't want you to be separated from God.

The myth says Hell is fun. It's an eternal party with all my friends. Other myths of Hell say it's only what we experience on this earth, or it isn't that bad.

There's the misconception that a loving God and an eternal Hell cannot coexist. Hell cannot be real if God really loves us.

But then there's the truth. The truth is that God loves you and I. He gave His only Son to die a horrific death in our place on the cross. That death took care of the punishment and gave us what we need to be able to stand before God without sin. All we have to do is place our faith and trust in Him. Our destination was not supposed to be Hell—we were created to be with God.

My question for you is this: Will you place your trust in Him? Jesus didn't stay dead. God raised Him from the dead, and He has been reunited with the Father, just as you can be. He wants to have a relationship with you. How will you accept that reality?

Christians are Stupid
Michael Laymon

Stupid: "Lacking ordinary quickness and keenness of mind. Dull, foolish, senseless, annoying, irritating."

You know what's interesting about the word *stupid*? It's probably the first bad word we learned, and we use it for all kinds of things that frustrate us. When we're trying to fix something and it won't cooperate, it becomes stupid. All kinds of technology—these complex devices become "stupid" when they don't work properly.

A common misconception about Christians is that we're stupid. People may think we're ignorant, narrow-minded, or just less intelligent. They think we are missing something up there in our brains because of what we believe.

But a lot of this frustration that people have with "stupid" Christians is not as much about what Christians lack as it is about the people not being able to get Christianity to work in a way they understand. It's like that malfunctioning computer—it's obviously not stupid. It's just confusing us, and we can't get it to do what we want. Since people can't figure it out, or it's not working in a way that's helpful, they call Christianity "stupid."

But Christianity isn't stupid, and I want to show you not only where this misconception comes from but also how we can better present our very non-stupid faith.

Let's first look at a couple reasons why Christianity doesn't make sense to people. **The first reason people think Christians are stupid is this: Many Christians today are not able to clearly articulate what they believe and why they believe it.** We may be trying to share our faith, and someone asks us a question, but we can't answer it. The reasons we can't answer vary; maybe we lack Biblical knowledge in a certain area, or maybe we don't want to cause trouble. Maybe we want to be more tolerant of other people's views or not scare them with a confident answer. And sometimes the answers we give just don't make sense to non-Christians.

I read something on a forum online that I want to share with you:

> As a child, I naively imagined that religion was all about love and spreading love. But as I grew older and watched some of the most ignorant people God ever created, I realized that for them, religion is nearly a cult and they are only concerned with people who think like them. This is not a rant against all Christians, nor is it a rant against all religion. However, there are some things that many Christians in America have been doing and saying that make them look very, very stupid. One of them is that Christians sound stupid when they say, "God wants me to spread His message of love to everyone." It's always comical and frustrating when I hear lunatics talk about God and what He's told them to do, which usually involves infringing on someone else's rights. It also typically involves spreading the word of a specific religion, not the pure word that God is love. Another statement that makes Christians sounds stupid is, "Unless a person is saved, they are damned to Hell." When you say that to another person who doesn't share your beliefs, you are probably the one who will be damned to Hell. Again, God doesn't need puny little mortals to force other mortals to believe in Him. People can find Jesus. Is He lost? If He is the Son of God, can't He very well find all of God's children by Himself?

The writer here talks about Christians being ignorant in a very compelling way. As he wraps this thing up, he says this:

> *If Christians are really concerned about God, then why not represent God without all of the other noise? Why can't it be about God, which is universal, as opposed to the Trinity and all the other things that are about religion and not really about universal spirituality? See, really, if any of us are really children of God and truly want to represent the love of God for mankind, then we would want to be about the business of finding more ways to be unified with each other as opposed to dividing. If I am a Muslim and you speak only of your love for God, then we can love God together. But once you speak of how I will be damned if I don't accept Jesus Christ as my Lord and Savior, you start to lose me, and the work of the devil begins. ... Now of course, some Muslims and some Jews are also zealous in their pursuit of religion and in being such are stupidly working against our purposeful existence, but since Christians are the majority, and since the nation was founded by people who placed Christian symbology with its very foundation, then Christians are the most prolific and stupidly overt religion. As opposed to alleged religious freedom the Pilgrims were pursuing, today stupid Christians want everyone to embrace one religion, and that's just stupid.*

This guy, I believe, speaks to how a lot of people think. Christians don't make sense.

Now, the reason we have trouble articulating what we believe is not because it's difficult to summarize. Christopher Hitchens, one of the world's most famous atheists, said this in an interview with a Unitarian minister:

I would say that if you don't believe that Jesus of Nazareth was the Christ and Messiah, and that He rose again from the dead and by His sacrifice our sins are forgiven, you're really not in any meaningful sense a Christian.

He knows what we're supposed to believe! So, if someone knows clearly what we believe but is still an atheist, there must be other reasons people think Christians are stupid—other than our not being able to articulate what we believe. The reason people think Christians are stupid goes deep.

I believe it is associated with the intentional, calculated anti-Christian campaign that is happening in the world today. You can see it in education, in politics, in entertainment, and in music. There is a strong attack today against Christians and the Christian belief system. People look at Christians and say they are stupid because what we believe and how we live is to them irrational, illogical, and judgmental. The culture of our country, from our school systems to our common opinion, has put Christian beliefs next to myths, backward thinking, and fear-oriented ignorance. They think we're clinging to something crazy and that we want to use it only to judge them.

As you can see, this goes back to the other reason of Christians not being able to explain their views well. We've failed to share the truth with people in a way they can understand, and the presentation we give them is sometimes alarming. They think we're crazy, or stupid, and it's no wonder they campaign against Christianity and the people who follow Jesus Christ.

But we've also got to understand that, even if we could explain Christianity in the clearest way, it's still going to be attacked. Christianity is very convicting. People are always going to want to discredit something that asks them to change their lives.

Think about the famous entertainers that attack Christianity. They are saying many of the same things as the author we just read. If you listen to many music artists and actors today, you'll hear a real hatred toward Christianity—and often a distortion of what Christians believe, to make Christians look stupid. You may say, "All right, these people are radical—they're really crazy," but they have a voice, and they are being heard.

People want to agree with what these entertainers are saying because it gives them a free pass to keep living the way they are living. The Bible talks about how Satan is orchestrating this attack against Christianity and how people side with it because they don't want to lose control of their lives.

If people believe that Jesus Christ is the Son of God, that God is, and that His Word is infallible and true, then they need to take into account and live by what He says to them. People can't acknowledge this truth and not do anything with it.

That's the key with the "Christians are stupid" thing: Other people don't believe, and we do. I'm not talking about head knowledge—knowing certain facts or arguments. Think about Christopher Hitchens—he "knows" what Christians believe, but he doesn't really know it. The knowledge a Christian has goes beyond intellect to the very heart and soul of life. It changes everything that we are. People who see the truth are left with two options: They've got to accept it and see their lives change—see themselves come under the control of God—or they need to find a way to say that truth isn't real, to discredit it, so they don't have to change.

The problem isn't the truth; it's that God's truth changes lives, and that's a much bigger issue for people than just acknowledging that Christianity makes sense.

So, now that we know the reasons why people think Christianity is stupid, let's look at what that means for us. Can anything be done to help people see God's truth—to show them Christianity is true and makes sense? The Bible has those answers.

If we want to help people get God's truth, we have to figure out whether we can even get truth at all. That may sound funny, but a common view today is agnosticism. That's the idea that we can't really know if there is a God, and if there is, there's no way we could know Him anyway. He'd be way too smart for us. We couldn't have a relationship with Him.

These people are saying that truth is too hard to discover, so we're crazy to suggest we've found it. But the Bible blows that claim apart. A big theme in the Bible is that God makes a point of communicating with us and showing us His truth. In fact, that's what makes Christianity different from all other religions—that God communicates with His followers through His Word and His Son, Jesus Christ.

Amos 4:13 tells us that God shares His thoughts with us: "For behold, He who forms mountains, And creates the wind, Who declares to man what his thought is, And makes the morning darkness, Who treads the high places of the earth— The LORD God of hosts is His name." We can know the truth, and it is not a question of how smart we are—it's what God shows us.

These verses make it clear that we *can* know God. So, our next question is, why don't more people trust God? What's the problem? Why don't we all have an understanding of God?

Our answer to this has to go back to human nature. When man was created, he communicated freely with God. But after the Fall, that communication became difficult because of sin. A barrier immediately went up, blocking what we know of God. As a result, it's no longer natural for us to see God working around us. It's not easy to know Him. Finding God and His knowledge requires effort—we have to work at it.

Paul writes about this in 1 Corinthians 1:18: "For the message of the cross is foolishness to those who are perishing, but to us who are being saved it is the power of God." God's truth isn't supposed to instantly make sense to us. We have gone so far from this truth in our years of sin. We need God's help to come back to truth, to realize what it means.

Paul says that not only does God's truth seem crazy to us, but the wisest people in the world often miss it. They're trying so hard to pull together all the loose ends that they don't look at the One behind it all and His simple message. Look at verses 20-21: "Where is the wise? Where is the scribe? Where is the disputer of this age? Has not God made foolish the wisdom of this world? For since, in the wisdom of God, the world through wisdom did not know God, it pleased God through the foolishness of the message preached to save those who believe."

What these verses are saying is that God didn't write down an authoritative, logical argument that would make sense to every person so they'd all accept Him. Instead, He gives us all His simple truth and asks us to believe. This truth is so basic, it looks like "foolishness"—like it can't possibly be right.

Think about your life—have you seen any examples of this? Can you think of any people who get their brains all twisted into knots trying to figure out the entire universe? God says His truth is surprisingly simple, but we have to look at Him—not ourselves—for it.

In 1 Corinthians chapter 2, Paul has some incredible thoughts. Now, remember Paul was one of the smartest guys of his time. He had the best schooling and knew what all the wise men thought. In these verses, he is talking about his ministry of sharing the Gospel with others. 1 Corinthians 2:1–5 says:

> "And I, brethren, when I came to you, did not come with excellence of speech or of wisdom declaring to you the testimony of God. For I determined not to know anything among you except Jesus Christ and Him crucified. I was with you in weakness, in fear, and in much trembling. And my speech and my preaching were not with persuasive words of human wisdom, but in demonstration of the Spirit and of power, that your faith should not be in the wisdom of men but in the power of God."

Paul tossed all the arguments and persuasive speeches out the window and just told people about Christ. It was not human wisdom but rather God's power that helped people understand Him. Verses 6–10 say:

> "However, we speak wisdom among those who are mature, yet not the wisdom of this age, nor of the rulers of this age, who are coming to nothing. But we speak the *wisdom* of God in a mystery, the hidden wisdom which God ordained before the ages for our glory, which none of the rulers of this age knew; for had they known, they would not have crucified the Lord of glory. But as it is written: '*Eye has not seen, nor ear heard, Nor have entered into the heart of man the things which God has*

prepared for those who love Him.' But God has revealed them to us through His Spirit. For the Spirit searches all things, yes, the deep things of God."

God's wisdom just won't make sense to people who have not experienced a changed heart, the faith that comes from believing in God. Paul was saying these people were missing out on truth because they were looking to themselves, not God. So, if we want to help people get God's truth—and further debunk this idea that Christians are crazy—that's where it starts: God.

The process of knowing God, whether it gets to the point of salvation, always starts in the same place. People must choose to believe. Now, real faith in God is a huge thing. For some people, it can take a lifetime to really trust God. But the process and the result are the same—belief. For some people, it may just start with them saying, "OK, I can accept that God might exist" or "OK, I believe the Bible is true." That first step of belief is where God works.

We see this a lot in our personal Christian walks. God tells us truth about Himself in the Bible, but we have to believe it before He can use it in our lives and help us have more knowledge. For example, Christians have been taught since they were young that God is sovereign—that He is in control. Now, we can know that in our heads, but until we really choose to believe it, not much is going to happen. When we finally trust God—when we say, "OK, God, I really believe You're in control," then He starts working. He shows us all these ways He really *is* in control. And we start to realize that a word like "sovereign," which was once just on a checklist of "the attributes of God," is a real, living concept that affects how we live. God gives us more knowledge, we trust Him again, and the cycle keeps going—at least, that's how it's supposed to work. (Why it's so hard to trust God is a discussion for another day!)

So, when it comes to the question of where we get God's truth, the answer starts with faith. People need to believe that what God says is true.

This is where the catch really is. If there's one thing people like more than being in control, it's trusting themselves. Your friend has the directions and is telling you to turn left, but you just *know* that you should keep going straight. Someone is giving you advice about a certain college, but you want to try it out yourself. People hate trusting stuff they're not sure about. Why should they gamble on Christianity? What if it's not true?

Being a Christian has a lot of risks, and people want to know what they're getting into if they're going to trust it. Worse yet, because of the two reasons we looked at before—that Christians don't know how to articulate their beliefs and that Christians are under attack—many people have no clue what they're being asked to believe.

Many people think faith is just believing in something without having any evidence. They think it's just going out on a limb without any assurance that they're going to find anything.

But the Bible isn't asking us to make irrational choices. Hebrews 11:1 says, "Now faith is the substance of things hoped for, the evidence of things not seen." That means that when we believe, we're "hoping for" something definite. We've been given "evidence" of what we can't see. The Bible doesn't say, "Believe in God, and hope you're OK when it's all over!" No way! All throughout the Bible are clear examples of what we can expect. Whether it's spiritual fruit that God promises us if we have faith (see Romans 5:1–5, James 1:2–6, 2 Peter 1:5–7), or the physical promises of Heaven that we can anticipate. Our faith is not pointed at systems or rules like, "I think if I always do right, people should help me out" or "I have faith in this sturdy chair, that it is the strongest and will hold me up." Our faith is based on a God Who holds the universe together and is always in control. We base our belief in a person Who has lived this life of faith before, Who has sent the Holy Spirit to help people believe despite their sinfulness.

The belief that God asks for is, first, rooted in Who He is, and second, amplified by the many specific promises He gives us in His Word. The Bible shows over and over again what the result of belief is. **When God asks us to trust, He is asking us to believe truth He has already shown us, with the promises that once we believe, we'll see even more.**

Even with all these promises, though, many people still have trouble with the Bible and belief because a lot of the Christian life can't be seen. To them, many parts of the Bible still don't make sense. Now, even though God doesn't ask us to base our beliefs on physical proof of Him (which He says throughout the Bible comes and goes with time), He has left us with some tangible examples that show that He and the Bible are true. For people who struggle with what seems like a lack of physical examples that Christianity is true, we do have some examples.

The Bible helps us understand the world around us—it backs up what we already know. Take science, for example. For centuries, science has tried to disprove the Bible. You know what's amazing? The Bible is continually affirming what science is discovering. Did you know that the world was once covered with water? Doesn't the Bible tell us that? Doesn't the Bible tell us that the stars are innumerable, and doesn't the Bible tell us that life is in the blood? Science has also discovered these truths.

How about history? There are historical records of the life of Jesus Christ. History recorded the prophecies He fulfilled. We have physical proof of many things the Bible says, and there's even philosophical proof that backs up key principles in the Bible.

All these things—science, nature, wisdom—back up what God has already said about Who He is. That means that His Word and what He asks us to believe is relevant. He should be our first stop for knowledge and wisdom—we don't have to wait for history and science to discover it!

If you think people have only recently become skeptical of God and His truth, think again. Think about when Jesus came to earth. All the Pharisees do throughout the four gospels is question Jesus—"How do we know you're real? Where's the proof? Why can't we keep living the way we're living?" Jesus gave them great spiritual answers, exposing their sin and their need for change, but He also gave them strong philosophical arguments—and tons of miracles. He used every example a person could want. The Pharisees could no longer say, "You didn't give me a reason to believe," because the answer was living right in front of them.

It wasn't irrational. It wasn't illogical. It was truth that was shown directly to them by what He had said and by what He had done. They could call Him stupid all they wanted, but it was their choice to believe. The Bible disproves people's argument that they shouldn't believe because there's no evidence. Clearly, there's plenty of evidence, and in many varieties. Most people may not get the whole picture of Who God is or how He's proven Himself, but they have enough to make a choice. They know some truth about God. So, even when people are faced with the truth, why don't they believe?

This answer goes back to the same reason people think Christians are stupid: They don't want to change. The way the world works is that people collect knowledge, and they look at it, and then maybe they decide what they believe. Jesus says to flip it around—come to Him in faith first. But to many people, that is too much. They want every detail proved first. Or worse, they don't ever want to give up control of their lives even when they know they're wrong.

So, we're back to the beginning. We know why people are opposed to Christianity, but we now also know that the only way to get them past this—taking them to the knowledge of God and pointing to belief—is exactly what they're opposed to! So, what do we do? Realizing how people respond to the truth, how should we present Christianity? It starts with what Paul said, how our faith is not about having a superior intellect. As we've just seen, the Bible has plenty of evidence—but that's not making anyone change. Evidence will help people get there, but it's the power of God that does the real work. It's not about being smarter than others. It *is* about the impact of God's Word in our lives. God has changed our hearts and changed who we are. The Bible says the power of God is this—not good arguments or being smart—it's showing people our lives are different!

Think back to what that first author said. Sure, he thought a lot of Christianity was stupid, but did you see what else he was saying? His other message was, "If you guys really have it all, why aren't your lives different? Why isn't this truth changing the world? Where's the Jesus-like love? Where's the power that changes lives?"

If we believe, and we continue to trust based on the truth God gives us, our lives should be changing. Our "main argument"—our answer to "Christians are stupid"—is "Sure, we look crazy—but you're not going to find this change anywhere else. No other religion or way of thinking can make lives different like Christ can."

People don't like to change, but this is good change. This change makes them the kind of people they want to be, the kind they've tried to be on their own but can't become without God's help. As we show them God's change, God will work in them to help them realize they need and want that change.

Some people suggest that Christians should be more tolerant—you know, act like we're OK with things so people will be more comfortable. But does that make sense? Christ's way of thinking is so crazy to the world that it would take a lot of adjusting for people to feel comfortable!

If people have to change, they'll oppose it, and the whole point of Christianity is that it's life-changing. So we have to stick to what God has said is true and trust that He will show these people they need Him. Tolerance won't solve their problems.

God knows that doing this won't be easy for us. 1 John 3:13 says, "Do not marvel, my brethren, if the world hates you." Don't be surprised. There will be people who will not like who you are, who will not like what you believe, who will not like what it means to them.

1 John 5:19 echoes this: "We know that we are of God, and the whole world lies under the sway of the wicked one." People who don't know Christ are locked into this other style of thinking.

The best thing we can do is to point other people and ourselves back to the source of knowledge, belief, and change: Jesus Christ. You see, it's easy for us to look at other people who aren't changing, who think Christians are stupid, and say that they need the help. But God is still working on changing us. We're always in the process of learning more and trusting, learning more and trusting. Before we can learn how to work with others, or see God use our example to lead them to Him, we need to be changing.

Look at Matthew 16:13–15. Jesus was with His disciples, and He said to them, "When Jesus came into the region of Caesarea Philippi, He asked His disciples, saying, 'Who do men say that I, the Son of Man, am?' So they said, 'Some say John the Baptist, some Elijah, and others Jeremiah or one of the prophets.' He said to them, 'But who do you say that I am?'"

That's a good question. Who do you say that Jesus is? Who is He to you?

That is the defining truth. That is what changes people's lives. Who do we say Jesus is?

Peter looked at Jesus and said, "You are the Christ, the Son of the living God." He knew Jesus couldn't be just another thing in his life, another guy he met, an add-on he could be comfortable with. He knew that Jesus had *changed everything*.

That's an important question for you today. Are you willing to accept Who Jesus says He is? Are you willing to let Him change you?

Today is your opportunity. If you don't know Christ as your personal Savior, this means taking that first step of faith we looked at before. Trust what God says, that He is the way of truth and salvation, and let Him change your life. Ask God to save you and show you more of Him. Ask Him to help you understand all those things about Him and Christianity that don't make sense.

Now, if you're a Christian, you may think, "Ah, I'm already saved—I don't have to look at any of this." Think for a minute, though: Can you say your life has been *changed* by Christ? You may be saved, but have you ever seen serious change in your life? Do you see God working in your life to give you understanding and develop your faith?

Remember, it's good to have evidence for Christianity ready so you can share it with people, but remember that our focus needs to be on Who Jesus is. He gave great arguments, and He did miracles; but those things weren't the point. They only directed people to the real reason He was here—to change lives, to show people truth.

Now, what should we expect once we do all this? This shouldn't come as a surprise, but even if we are prepared, even if we have the right answers, even if we manage to live in a Christ-like way, the attack isn't going to stop. John said, "Hey, don't be surprised if the world hates you." But I can tell you this: you can still be a light in the midst of that attack. It's going to come from all sides, but you can still be used by God in the midst of that attack to lead people to Him.

We need to be preparing ourselves to share truth as Christ would, with a loving attitude that sees where people are coming from. Have you heard the phrase "compassion for the lost"? "The lost"—we hear that term a lot. Think about it. These people are *lost*, confused. They don't know their way out of where they are. They have incomplete head knowledge—they can't figure out where to find hope and meaning and real life. They need someone to be kind and caring as they are led to the truth.

As we prepare to point people to God's truth, we can be sure of what we're doing. We know God, and we know that this comes from the experience of faith in Christ. Through faith in God, He shows us over and over again that He's doing a work in our lives. We see this work every day, and as He works in us, we come to know Him more. This change, this wisdom, surpasses any textbook knowledge. This is as far opposite of "stupid" as you can be. There is no greater truth. There is no greater knowledge than knowing Jesus Christ. You know all this, but who else is missing out?

chapter 7

Christians are Hypocrites
Ric Garland

When you were younger, did you believe in monsters? Did you think there were monsters under your bed? I'll be honest. I thought there were monsters and all that. I was always afraid to sleep with my hand over the side of my bed. I was afraid that something would happen in the middle of the night when everything was quiet, that whatever was underneath my bed would grab my hand and drag me underneath and I would never be seen again. It scared the life out of me. I was totally afraid.

I can tell you today, though, that I do not believe in monsters. I think they are ridiculous. But you know what? I still can't sleep with my hand over the side of my bed.

Have you ever feared something like that? Are you paranoid about anything?

Paranoia is being afraid of something. It's not logical, but those fears are very real. For instance, I hate heights. I hate heights! I hate being in tall places. I used to live in Florida, and there is a very tall bridge there called the Sunshine State Bridge. When I would drive over it, my heart would start pounding faster and faster. Something in me would say, "The wind is going to blow you off. You're going to go over the side. It's over."

Now, I could do a report on that bridge. I could look up who made it and all the reasons it's safe. I could look at the total number of people who have crossed it without dying. In my head, I can know it's safe. But when I go to cross it, I'm still going to be shaking and sweating. It's the same thing with the monsters—I'm "sure" they don't exist, but you're not going to catch me with my hand hanging over the side of the bed. You know what this is? It's my behavior betraying what I say I really believe. I know one thing in my head, but my body is doing something else.

This is where the fear of monsters and fear of heights come into Christianity. Too often, behavior betrays belief.

I'm going to ask you some questions. Be honest. Do you know another Christian young person who lies? How about one who cheats? How about one who steals? One who gossips? One who disobeys his or her parents? Disrespects authority? Curses? Smokes? Does illegal drugs? Gets drunk? Looks at porn? Has sex? Had an abortion? How about has a daily quiet time? Memorizes Scripture (by his or her own choice)? Shares the Gospel regularly? Lives a consistent Christian lifestyle?

Let me tell you what I have discovered. You know more Christians that lie, cheat, and disobey their parents than have a quiet time. You know more Christians that curse, smoke, and get drunk than memorize Scripture. You know more Christians who look at porn and have sex than share the Gospel. You know almost as many Christians that take drugs illegally than live a consistent Christian lifestyle. Talk about hypocrisy. These questions show it. We know people who say they love God and that they are Christians, but they lie, cheat, have sex, and look at porn. I know more Christians who do that than have a quiet time, memorize Scripture, and live a consistent Christian lifestyle.

What is hypocrisy? A basic definition is this: *A hypocrite is a person whose behavior doesn't match what he says he believes.* The word *hypocrite* comes from the Greek culture. It is derived from someone who plays a part on stage. The person would play a part that was totally different from what he or she was like in real life, or sometimes that person would play more than one part. The performer would wear different masks for the different parts. That's where the saying "two-faced" comes from. This person was two-faced, having two parts, being a hypocrite.

A big word in today's culture is *authenticity*. We don't want to be sold something that isn't real. We don't like things that come off as insincere. We want something that's genuine; we want something that's real.

I'm not going to surprise you when I say that religious people tend to be the biggest hypocrites out there. You can probably think of thousands of examples. How about church leaders who preach one thing, then do another? Do you have any friends who act one way at church and another way at school? How about you? Do you ever have trouble living out what's right?

Hypocrites have been around a long time. As long as there's been truth, there have been people teaching it but not living it. Jesus Christ ran into a lot of these hypocrites. Do you know how He responded? In Matthew 23, He speaks to the religious leaders of His time. They knew God's truth but were living something else. Jesus calls them hypocrites six times in Matthew 23:13, 14, 15, 23, 25, 27 by saying, "Woe to you, scribes and Pharisees, hypocrites!" He didn't stutter. He laid it out there. He said, "You religious leaders—you are phonics, hypocrites." I want to take you to Scripture and show you two kings. Both of them are hypocrites. The first king I want you to see is in 1 Samuel 15. Verses 1–3 say, "Samuel also said to Saul, 'The LORD sent me to anoint you king over His people, over Israel. Now therefore, heed the voice of the words of the LORD. Thus says the LORD of hosts: I will punish Amalek for what he did to Israel, how he ambushed him on the way when he came up from Egypt. Now go and attack Amalek, and utterly destroy all that they have, and do not spare them. But kill both man and woman, infant and nursing child, ox and sheep, camel and donkey.'" Verse 9 reads: "But Saul and the people spared Agag and the best of the sheep, the oxen, the fatlings, the lambs, and all that was good, and were unwilling to utterly destroy them. But everything despised and worthless, that they utterly destroyed."

Did you get it? God says to destroy everything. Saul goes out and does not destroy everything. Huh.

Verse 13 says, "Then Samuel went to Saul, and Saul said to him, 'Blessed are you of the LORD! I have performed the commandment of the LORD.'" LIAR. He's a hypocrite. And he's happy about it. Here's the response in verses 14-26: "But Samuel said, 'What then is this bleating of the sheep in my ears, and the lowing of the oxen which I hear?' And Saul said, 'They have brought them from the Amalekites; for the people spared the best of the sheep and the oxen, to sacrifice to the LORD your God; and the rest we have utterly destroyed.' Then Samuel said to Saul, 'Be quiet! And I will tell you what the LORD said to me last night.' And he said to him, 'Speak on.' So Samuel said, 'When you were little in your own eyes, were you not head of the tribes of Israel? And did not the LORD anoint you king over Israel? Now the LORD sent you on a mission, and said, 'Go, and utterly destroy the sinners, the Amalekites, and fight against them until they are consumed.' Why then did you not obey the voice of the LORD? Why did you swoop down on the spoil, and do evil in the sight of the LORD?' And Saul said to Samuel, 'But I have obeyed the voice of the LORD, and gone on the mission on which the LORD sent me, and brought back Agag king of Amalek; I have utterly destroyed the Amalekites. But the people took of the plunder, sheep and oxen, the best of the things which should have been utterly destroyed, to sacrifice to the LORD your God in Gilgal.' So Samuel said: 'Has the LORD as great delight in burnt offerings and sacrifices, As in obeying the voice of the LORD? Behold, to obey is better than sacrifice, And to heed than the fat of rams. For rebellion is as the sin of witchcraft, And stubbornness is as iniquity and idolatry. Because you have rejected the word of the LORD, He also has rejected you from being king.' Then Saul said to Samuel, 'I have sinned, for I have transgressed the commandment of the LORD and your words, because I feared the people and obeyed their voice. Now therefore, please pardon my sin, and return with me, that I may worship the LORD.' But Samuel said to Saul, 'I will not return with you, for you have rejected the word of the

LORD, and the LORD has rejected you from being king over Israel.'"

What a hypocrite! Saul is king of Israel. God says, "Wipe out all the Amalekites. Everybody. Everything." Saul comes back and says to God's prophet, "Hi, Samuel. We did what God commanded." Samuel says, "Wait a minute. Why are there goats and sheep when God said to wipe out everything? Why is King Agag here when God said everyone?" Saul says, "Well—well, we did everything God commanded."

No, he didn't. He didn't do it. Even when Saul is caught red-handed in a lie, he gives this reason: "Well, Samuel, I was pressured by all these people. I did it because they wanted to." He isn't willing to admit his mistake. A leader of God's people clearly and deliberately disobeys God's command. Do you think that all the people saw that? If God lets it go, what message will He be sending to the people? What message will He be sending to others? Do you think people will respect God and His prophets?

Because of Saul's disobedience and unwillingness to own up to his own sin, God removes his family from being a dynasty in Israel.

Here's one more verse. Look at Saul's response: "Then he said, 'I have sinned; *yet* honor me now, please, before the elders of my people and before Israel, and return with me, that I may worship the LORD your God.'" Saul wants to make it better. But God knows that even if Saul does the right thing this time, he isn't doing it for the right reason. He still doesn't believe. Saul wants to change his behavior but not his beliefs. He wants to change his behavior to get what he wants, but he isn't willing to change his heart to be humble before God.

Let's look at a different king.

This one we find in 2 Samuel. It's King David. In 2 Samuel 11:1–5 it says,

> It happened in the spring of the year, at the time when kings go out to battle, that David sent Joab and his servants with him, and all Israel; and they destroyed the people of Ammon and besieged Rabbah. But David remained at Jerusalem. Then

it happened one evening that David arose from his bed and walked on the roof of the king's house. And from the roof he saw a woman bathing, and the woman was very beautiful to behold. So David sent and inquired about the woman. And someone said, 'Is this not Bathsheba, the daughter of Eliam, the wife of Uriah the Hittite?' Then David sent messengers, and took her; and she came to him, and he lay with her, for she was cleansed from her impurity; and she returned to her house. And the woman conceived; so she sent and told David, and said, 'I am with child.'

David gets the same treatment as Saul. A prophet comes, sent from God. 2 Samuel 12:1–14 says,

Then the LORD sent Nathan to David. And he came to him, and said to him: 'There were two men in one city, one rich and the other poor. The rich man had exceedingly many flocks and herds. But the poor man had nothing, except one little ewe lamb which he had bought and nourished; and it grew up together with him and with his children. It ate of his own food and drank from his own cup and lay in his bosom; and it was like a daughter to him. And a traveler came to the rich man, who refused to take from his own flock and from his own herd to prepare one for the wayfaring man who had come to him; but he took the poor man's lamb and prepared it for the man who had come to him.' So David's anger was greatly aroused against the man, and he said to Nathan, 'As the LORD lives, the man who has done this shall surely die! And he shall restore fourfold for the lamb, because he did this thing and because he had no pity.' Then Nathan said to David, 'You are the man! Thus says the LORD God of Israel: 'I anointed you king over Israel, and I delivered you from the hand of Saul. I gave you your master's house and your master's wives into your keeping, and gave you the house of Israel and Judah. And if that had been too little, I also would have given you much more! Why have you despised the commandment of the LORD, to do evil in His sight? You have killed Uriah the Hittite with the sword; you have taken his wife to be your wife, and have killed him with the sword of the people of Ammon. Now therefore, the sword shall never depart from your house, because you have despised Me, and have taken the wife of Uriah the Hittite to be your wife.' Thus says the LORD: 'Behold, I will raise up adversity against you from your own house; and I will take your wives before your eyes and give them to your neighbor, and he shall lie with your wives in the sight of this sun. For you did it secretly, but I will do this thing before all Israel, before the sun." So David said to Nathan, 'I have sinned against the LORD.' And Nathan said to David, 'The LORD also has put away your sin; you shall not die. However, because by this deed you have given great occasion to the enemies of the LORD to blaspheme, the child also who is born to you shall surely die.'

What a story. Here's David, king of Israel. His men are out at battle. He goes on top of the palace and looks around, and he sees Bathsheba taking a bath. He lusts after her. He has servants asks who she is. He has them bring her to the palace, and then he has sex with her. Here's the problem: She finds out she is pregnant. David now tries to cover up his sin. He brings Uriah, Bathsheba's husband, home from battle to see if he will have sex with her to cover up the sin. But Uriah is such a man of integrity that he will not. The only way David can get rid of him is by killing him. He murders Uriah. Then he lies! He covers it up. He brings Bathsheba in, makes her his wife, and everything is "fine." Now think about that. For a whole year this is going on. For a whole year David thinks everything is cool. "I got away with my sin." But his servants know what happened. Don't you think they are talking? You better believe they are talking. All those servants start talking, and I'm sure it spreads all throughout Israel. "Hey, do you know what David did?" "Get what David did...." "Hey, this is the same David that wrote the Psalms, the same David who killed Goliath. The same David who says he loves God. Man, look what he did. He had sex with this woman, had her husband killed, and took her in and covered it up. He's pretending like everything is fine." Isn't that amazing? For a year it goes on, and it spreads around. This is pretty much as bad as hypocrisy can get.

But look at this. In Acts 13:22, centuries after David lived, the writer says, "And when He had removed him, He raised up for them David as king, to whom also He gave testimony and said, '*I have found David the son of Jesse, a man after My own heart, who will do all My will.*'" In Acts, God calls David a man after His own heart. This is a man who committed adultery. This is a man who committed murder. This is a man who lived a hypocritical life and misled a nation. God calls him a man after His own heart and sets up his lineage as a dynasty. When Saul disobeyed God, God said, "That's it, I'm going to remove him." Saul apologized—he tried to make it up. But it was over.

What's the difference? Why the difference? Let me tell you what I think. When Saul was confronted with his sin, he made excuses. He eventually was sorry, but only after being punished. He wouldn't humble himself before God. When David was confronted, he confessed his sins in true repentance.

Here's the bottom line. You may be reading this and thinking, "Man, I don't want to be a Christian. They're all hypocrites. They say they love God and follow the Bible, but they don't. They're always spreading hurt and being fake." Well, you've got part of it right. All of us, in one degree or another, live an inconsistent life. But here's the point: When we, as Christians, are confronted with the truth of the Word of God, what do we do about it? Saul just made excuses; David changed his beliefs and his behavior. David changed his mind. He repented of his sin.

That's what we need to be looking for in ourselves. Yes, we're going to mess up. But how do we respond?

James MacDonald wrote a great book called *I Really Want to Change, So Help Me God*. He gives us good instructions on what real repentance looks like. He gives four fruits of repentance—four ways we can know we are really repenting.

First, there is an absence of rationalization. There's none of this, "Well, it's hard for me," or "Man, you don't understand my parents." Excuses. When you repent, excuses become disgusting. You know exactly how wrong you've been and how nothing gets you off the hook. When you truly repent, when you stop being a hypocrite, you stop rationalizing. You're not searching for excuses. You're just making it right.

Second, there's genuine sorrow. You understand that when you are being a hypocrite, you are disappointing God. This sorrow is on your mind when you think about your sin—how you have made God feel.

Third is open confession of sin. See, David hid his sin of adultery until he repented. But people who are genuinely repentant don't care who knows because they've done business with a holy God. They say, "Man, you know what? I know I'm a filthy, rotten, wicked sinner, but praise God, I have His grace in my life." They know God is changing them. And as part of that change, they want people to know they don't want sin to be a part of their lives. They aren't OK just fixing themselves and fixing their relationship with God—they have to make it up to the people they hurt.

The last fruit is restitution: "I'll make things right." They try to correct the wrong they've done, give back to the people they've hurt.

Do you realize that repentance is a gift from God? He doesn't want us to continually be broken over our sin just so we'll feel bad! He wants us to be humble and confess our sin so He can forgive us. He wants to have a relationship with us, which He can't do with a barrier of sin. When we repent, He forgives us and starts working again. We can be near Him once again.

Let me share with you what God does with a repenter's sin. Isaiah 43:25 says, "I, even I, am He who blots out your transgressions for My own sake; And I will not remember your sins." Micah 7:18–19 says, "Who is a God like You, Pardoning iniquity And passing over the transgression of the remnant of His heritage? He does not retain His anger forever, Because He delights in mercy. He will again have compassion on us, And will subdue our iniquities. You will cast all our sins Into the depths of the sea." Acts 3:19 says, "Repent therefore and be converted, that your sins may be blotted out, so that times of refreshing may come from the presence of the Lord" In our repentance, God completely forgives us and gets rid of our sin. He brings us back to Him. He refreshes us.

In this book we're talking about reasons people aren't Christians. In this chapter, we covered a big one—because people think Christians are hypocrites. So what are we going to do with what we've seen here? The myth says all Christians are hypocrites, and God does not care. But is that what the Bible shows us? No—God does care. Jesus called out the Pharisees. God sent prophets to confront Saul and David. Some

Christians may be hypocrites, but that doesn't reflect on God. God wants us to live righteously, and He will step in when we don't. This myth doesn't work—that God doesn't care if people are hypocrites.

"OK," you say. "Fine. God cares. But that doesn't mean I want to be a Christian. There are so many rules and regulations. I don't want to be a hypocrite." But this way of thinking is off, too—it's a misconception. Christianity is not about rules. It's a relationship. When you become a Christian, you're not signing up to follow a list of instructions. What you're doing is going into a relationship with Jesus Christ. He guides you, He loves you; you follow Him, you trust Him. And when you mess up, there's the gift of repentance—saying you're wrong and asking Him to patch it up. Christianity is not about people perfectly living a system of beliefs. It's a friendship, and sometimes a friend disappoints a friend, but that's no reason to throw out the relationship altogether. The misconception says "Don't be a Christian because you can't do it." God's truth says "Be a Christian because Christ will do it."

We've disproved the myth that God doesn't care about hypocritical behavior, the misconception that Christians can't help but be hypocrites. All we have left now is the truth. So, what do we do now?

First of all, let's look at Christians. If you are a Christian, did it ever occur to you that sometimes, because of the way you are living your life, you are influencing others who are not saved? Maybe you are reading this and you have to admit, "Hey, I'm a hypocrite." <I love what LaCrae said in his music video that he was just talking about the fact that, "Hey, I know a guy that is struggling. That guy that I'm praying for, it's me. I'm the man." Maybe he would say to you ladies that you are the one that is struggling.> May I give you a suggestion? Change.

I love Psalm 51 because it was written by David after his confession of sin to the prophet Nathan. Verses 1–2 start with the confession of sin: "Have mercy upon me, O God, According to Your lovingkindness; According to the multitude of Your tender mercies, Blot out my transgressions. Wash me thoroughly from my iniquity, And cleanse me from my sin." David calls his sin three things. He calls it *transgression*—an act of rebellion. He calls it *iniquity*—a crooked or perverse act. He calls it *sin*, missing the mark. He says, "God, I'm not making excuses any longer. I'm not going to rationalize. I have transgressed, I have committed iniquity, I have sinned. It's me." Then he says, "God, I want you to blot it out." He wants Him to erase it from his records. He wants to be completely cleaned out. He wants to be whole again. In verse 10, he asks God to restore his passion. He says, "Create in me a clean heart, O God, And renew a steadfast spirit within me." He had become apathetic and indifferent to sin. He wants the passion back.

Look at verse 12: "Restore to me the joy of Your salvation, And uphold me by Your generous Spirit." Verse 13 says, "Then I will teach transgressors Your ways, And sinners shall be converted to You." He wants a pure heart again (v. 10), a powerful ministry (v. 11), and joy in God's salvation (v. 12). In verse 13, he's saying, "Look, God, forgive me, and I will then help others." Do you know what the beautiful thing in the Christian life is? We are all struggling. We don't have it all together. We don't have it all perfect. We all live like hypocrites at points. But we have the choice to hope and pray that the Spirit of God will take the Word of God and expose these areas in our lives that should be changed. God will change us, and He will use us to help others.

A man fell into a pit once, and he couldn't get out. He started calling out for help. As he did, a religious man came by. The man said, "Sir, help me, help me!" The religious man wrote a prayer and threw it down to him and said, "Here, pray this prayer." It didn't work, and the guy kept calling out for help. A lawyer came by and threw down his card that said, "When you get out, call me and we'll sue." As he kept calling, the man's best friend came by. He jumped in the pit with him. The guy said, "Now, what did you do that for? Now we're both stuck!" His best friend said, "No, I've been in here before, and I know the way out." You and I, as Christians, get to help others out of the pit by directing people to the Word of God and encouraging them by telling them how it can change lives.

Maybe you are reading this and you don't know Jesus Christ as your Savior. You've never made that choice. You're going, "Man, I just don't know." You've used the excuse, "All Christians are hypocrites." But what about Jesus? He demands authenticity and honesty. He will deal with those people for their actions, and He wants you to take care of yourself. You may have problems, you may have issues, but are you willing to come to Him? His arms are open, and He's gracious. He wants you to change what you think about Him. He wants a relationship. He wants you to come to Him and say, "Look, I've got problems, I've got issues, but I am willing to come and believe in You, Jesus Christ. I'm willing to come and say, 'I know that I'm a sinner. I know that I'm inconsistent, but I know that You can forgive my wrong and give me a relationship with you.'"

Would you come to Jesus Christ?

chapter 8

God is Mean
Mike Calhoun

You may be thinking, "Saying God is mean isn't the typical way to begin a chapter about God." But you've probably had similar thoughts about God. Sometimes the way things happen in this world, or what God does in the Bible, just makes Him look really mean. Is He a God of love? Is He kind? Or is He really mean and vindictive? Depending on who you're listening to, you'll hear both viewpoints.

You may be reading this and are not a Christian. The main reason you haven't wanted to become a Christian is because God doesn't seem to care. He seems like a mean, wrathful, unkind God who always wants to get His way, and you're not interested in that.

You're not crazy to wonder about God. Look at some of the things that are going on in the world. How do you explain what happened in Haiti? How do you explain the Chilean earthquake and other earthquakes? People dying, the suffering? How do you explain all that plus the evil in your own neighborhood? How do you weigh all that with God's love? You've heard people's answers. You've heard the clichés. God did it for this reason, or it's not bad because of this particular reason. What often happens is people try to explain it because they want to protect God's reputation. But do you know what? God doesn't need anyone to protect Him. He doesn't need human excuses. He doesn't need Christians to attempt to cover up for Him. He's OK as He is.

People have different reasons why they don't want to become a Christian. For some people, it's "I see Christians, and they're boring. They're boring because God is boring. God seems to be taking all their fun away and boxing them in. He's building this barrier around them so they can't really enjoy life. There are too many rules. And God judges all the people that don't agree with Him? That's just mean." I've met a lot of people who have thought that. But is that what really happens?

Let's see what the Bible says about it. Now, if I was God, and I had this book written, I would not have put all the bad parts in it. I mean, I would have told the story, and I would have made everything work out just right. I wouldn't have included some of the tragedy you read about in the Bible. For example, if I was God, I would never have included a book called Job. The book of Job is one of those parts you read and go, "Oh, man! Wait a minute. What's going on here?" If you're thinking of God being mean, let me give you a little fuel for your fire. Look at this story.

In Job, Satan approaches God, and he's been watching the people on earth. God says, "Have you considered My servant Job?" God looks at this Being that is causing trouble all over earth, and gives him a new target. Now, if God is really a loving God, He would protect His own children, wouldn't He? He wouldn't point them out to Satan, right?

In verse 8, God says to Satan, *"Then the LORD said to Satan, 'Have you considered My servant Job, that there is none like him on the earth, a blameless and upright man, one who fears God and shuns evil?'"* You would think, "Leave that guy alone—go get somebody else." But God actually calls Satan's attention to him. God isn't just making a suggestion. He's saying, "This guy is really righteous. I bet he can take your best stuff, Satan." Look what happens starting in verses 13-22:

Now there was a day when his sons and daughters were eating and drinking wine in their oldest brother's house; and a messenger came to Job and said, 'The oxen were plowing and the donkeys feeding beside them, when the Sabeans raided them and took them away—indeed they have killed the servants with the edge of the sword; and I alone have escaped to tell you!' While he was still speaking, another also came and said, 'The fire of God fell from heaven and burned up the sheep and the servants, and consumed them; and I alone have escaped to tell you!' While he was still speaking, another also came and said, 'The Chaldeans formed three bands, raided the camels and took them away, yes, and killed the servants with the edge of the sword; and I alone have escaped to tell you!' While he was still speaking, another also came and said, 'Your sons and daughters were eating and drinking wine in their oldest brother's house, and suddenly a great wind came from across the wilderness and struck the four corners of the house, and it fell on the young people, and they are dead; and I alone have escaped to tell you!' Then Job arose, tore his robe, and shaved his head; and he fell to the ground and worshiped. And he said: 'Naked I came from my mother's womb, And naked shall I return there. The LORD gave, and the LORD has taken away; Blessed be the name of the LORD.' In all this Job did not sin nor charge God with wrong.

I'm going to summarize it for you. Job is with a group of people, and a servant shows up and says a bunch of Job's animals—his way of making money—have been destroyed. While he's still talking, another guy comes in and says that fire torched more of his stuff. And then another guy comes and says even more of his livestock has been taken. And then the worst part—until now, it was all possessions and servants, but the last guy comes with the news that a big wind crushed the house where all Job's children were. Nothing survives—he doesn't even have a couple little goats to hang onto. All his possessions, all his wealth, and even his children are wiped out. He finds out in a space of a few minutes that it's all gone. Now, the book of Job tells us that Satan was behind this. It wasn't God destroying everything. But doesn't it still seem really mean that God let it happen? It's like He not only stood by and let a bully on the playground take all of the good kid's stuff and kick dirt in his face—but He also suggested that the bully do it. That doesn't seem right.

Notice that Job still has a great attitude toward God. But what is God's response? He tells Satan he can keep beating Job up! God gives Satan the green light again, and the only thing he isn't allowed to do is kill Job. Chapter 2 says Satan goes back and gives Job some painful sores all over his body, from the bottom of his feet to the top of his head. So this man who is godly and righteous and upright, who fears God and who hates sin, has lost everything. On top of that, now he's in incredible pain in all parts of his body.

If that isn't enough, three "friends" come. They have heard about Job's adversity. First, they sit and stare at Job for seven days. That will weird you out! They just sit and stare at him for seven days; nobody says a word. Still, that is probably the best time he is going to have with these friends, because when they do open their mouths, it's not good. You know what they say? One of them says, "I know what it is, Job. You have sinned." The other one just pounds him and pounds him with endless questions. The third one tells him his doctrine is wrong.

Here's a guy who has lost everything and who is suffering horribly. Instead of trying to encourage him, his friends are going, "You're a sinner," and the other one keeps throwing questions at him. When you're not feeling well, that's not the time to answer questions or have someone challenge your life. Job can barely move and is still dealing with all the deaths in his family, and these guys are here calling him out. Not only do they not comfort him; they add to his problems and heartache.

It can't get any worse. Job has *nothing* to hang onto—and he can't even just sit there and wallow. He has people pecking at him, making him suffer even more. When you look at the story of Job, it really looks like Job is a victim and that God is mean.

The issue we face is our perspective. The problem I have, and maybe you too, is that I usually turn most of my focus on myself and not on others—and not on God. I look at things in a way that makes sense to me. For example, think about God killing His only Son. No human would ever think that was a good idea—and especially not a loving one! From our perspective, that is always going to be strange and unloving.

We don't see it how God sees it, and that's why it's so hard for us.

Understanding why things happen is a big deal for us—we want to know why God is doing something before we are OK with it. But to be able to grasp some of these situations where God seems really mean, we've got to realize He is in control. He is sovereign. If we understand His perspective, we've got to realize that He does these things not because He's mean, but because He's loving, and they fit into His big picture somehow. We have finite minds and can only see so much, but He is infinite and can use situations in a lot of different ways.

You may be thinking, "Wait—you just jumped from God being mean to saying God is love, but I don't see the proof. I'm just supposed to accept that He's sovereign? You're saying God is love even if I can't see it, but how do you know that?" Think about Jesus' death again. This seems like an angry God, a mean God that deserts a good Person and just lets Him rot. But we know that through this death came the greatest show of God's love, the greatest good for all people. It looks mean until we see how it was a passing moment to a great act of love. And that's what we're getting at here—we see the effects of a "mean God," but we need to be looking for His greater love behind it.

Think about some of the stuff we said at the beginning of the chapter about why people don't want to be Christians—that Christians are boring, that God boxes them in and gives them a bunch of rules. That's certainly what it looks like from our perspective. But to get the big picture, let's look at an example that will help us understand how God sees it.

The Bible talks a lot about God being a Father to Christians, so let's use the example of parents and children as we think about the big picture of love that is behind what God does.

Think about a dad who keeps his toddler from running into the street, for example. Is that mean? Of course not! That's loving, even if the kid thinks his dad is the biggest killjoy ever. John 10:10 says, "The thief does not come except to steal, and to kill, and to destroy. I have come that they may have life, and that they may have it more abundantly." Satan is out to destroy people, to bring down Christians, and to keep everyone he can from God. He wants to steal, kill, and destroy life. God is the protection from that. And not only does He keep Satan away, He also offers a better life—an "abundant" existence. That is not boring!

The things God has to offer those who are truly his children are great, and so far better than regular life. But just like parents and children in real life, He can't just let His children run completely free and crazy. I'm sure you've seen this before. Some parents want their kids to be happy, so they spoil them or let them do whatever. But those kids end up having a lot of struggles. Parents who really love their kids are often involved and making sure they don't make poor choices.

God seems really confining, like His commandments will keep people from having fun or having a good life. Look at Psalm 119:45, though. It says, "And I will walk at liberty, For I seek Your precepts." The writer was saying that he found freedom when he studied God's Word, when he learned what God said was the best way to live.

God's instructions aren't meant to box us in; He gives them to us so we won't have to try a bunch of other ways that won't work. People who don't have God's guidelines are the ones who are tied down— they are trapped into having to keep trying things, hoping something will work and make them happy. God says He's done the work for us. He knows the best way to live. He has the shortcuts to freedom. In 2 Corinthians 3:17 it says, "Now the Lord is the Spirit; and where the Spirit of the Lord is,there is liberty." Galatians 5:1 says, "Stand fast therefore in the liberty by which Christ has made us free, and do not be entangled again with a yoke of bondage." Knowing the Word of God will release us. It doesn't restrict us.

Once I was speaking at a camp in the mountains of southern California near San Bernardino. I borrowed a car and went on a little excursion. If you've ever been out there you know that you can be driving along, and all of a sudden you're in front of a mountain. You keep driving and you just go right up. They have carved the roads out of the side of the mountain. Here I was, five or six thousand feet up. On one side is the mountain, and on the other side is air. That's it! As I'm driving along there, I notice these guardrails. I'm thinking, "What in the world? Who is trying to restrict my life? Don't they understand

I have the right to drive anywhere I want to? I mean, if I want to drive over there, that's my business. Somebody's trying to fence me in." Is that what you would have thought? No! Me neither, really. We'd think, "No, no, no. That's not a fence, that's a guardrail. That's for my protection."

It's the same thing with God. People criticize Him. They say, "He's building fences. He's restricting people." But those are guardrails to protect us. God knows that getting involved in sin will leave us unfulfilled. It will leave us with a warped mindset, living with a worldview that is completely distorted.

People accuse God of being mean. It almost looks like He is. Look at Job. If you were in Job's place, what would you do? Even if we still thought God was in control, we'd probably be saying, "This is not fair. This is not right. This is just mean." Listen to what Job does. He praises God. He says, "Naked I came from my mother's womb, And naked shall I return there." Then he says this: "The LORD gave, and the LORD has taken away; Blessed be the name of the LORD" (Job 1:21).

Here is a man who has lost everything, who is suffering greatly. Yet he still says, "I want to praise God." Somewhere along the way, he has gotten the proper perspective. He seems crazy, but remember that this is someone God pointed to when Satan challenged Him. This is God's prime example of a righteous man. So, he must have something figured out. But how did he get this way?

The key is understanding that the whole world is not about us. We often think that the way things happen are directly related to us. But there's a bigger picture here. Job doesn't blame God. Job 1:22 says, "In all this Job did not sin nor charge God with wrong." Job keeps the big picture in mind.

Look at the choices Job makes. Over and over He keeps choosing to keep the big picture in mind and to trust God. Job's wife even tells him, "Here's what I think you ought to do, Job. You need to curse God and die." She's like, "What's the point? This is too much. Just tell God what you think, that this isn't right." Look at Job's answer: "But he said to her, 'You speak as one of the foolish women speaks. Shall we indeed accept good from God, and shall we not accept adversity?'" Here's a man who has the right perspective about life. He knows he doesn't deserve all the good things he has from God any more than he deserves the bad he is getting. So he decides to just wait and let God do whatever.

Most of us, me included, look at life and say, "Hey look, you know what? I'm a believer; I'm Your child, after all—just give me the good stuff!" But Job says, "Can't I just take the good and the bad and trust God with both?"

If you read the book all the way through, in chapter 42, you'll notice something. After all the dialogue with Job's three friends, after he talks about knowing God and how he is committed to God, Job says, "Listen to me, I'm not going to go there, because God is God, and I am not. He has the right, and I don't. He understands the big picture, and I don't. I don't get it." Job says no matter what happens, he is OK letting God be God.

Chapter 42 says God blessed Job again. He gave Job more than he had in the beginning. Because Job's focus was on God, on the bigger picture, he got to see life from God's perspective. And physical blessings came after that. As you think about the bigger picture, why are you here? I said at the beginning of the chapter that if I were God, I would not have put the book of Job in the Bible. But after reading, studying, and evaluating it and seeing Job's life, I changed my mind. I would put it in, because here's a story of a man who realized his life had a purpose that was bigger than himself. All these years later we're still moved by the way Job approached life. "God can give me good; God can give me adversity. He's God, and I'm not." Job can say, "I was here." He lived this. He learned in a firsthand way that God had a purpose for him.

Job got a glimpse of the bigger picture when he chose to trust God. Notice that this didn't come instantly, though. Job had a long time of waiting and wondering and suffering. But what did he do in that time? He trusted God.

That's where I want us to start today. We know the truth—that God is in control, that He knows the big picture, and that what He's doing with us can be trusted because He loves us. What we have to do is come to a place where we determine whether we are going to trust the truth. I can't convince you to do that. I can't say, "If you do this, every single thing will be just right in your life." If somebody says to you, "Look, if you become a Christian, then everything will be great," they're wrong. That's not the point of being a Christian, of living life. There will be good, and there will be adversity. So, the bottom line is this: We have to come to a place of trusting.

We all trust someone. We all believe something. The person who says, "I don't believe in anything" or "I don't trust anybody" is the same person who will walk onto an airplane, strap themselves into a seat, and let someone fly him 500 miles per hour to somewhere. We all trust. We all believe. We just have to make the choice who and what we believe.

So, are you going to believe the myth? The myth is that God is mean, that God has too many rules, that God is boring. Are you going to buy into the misconception that because life is rough, you just have to do the best you can and enjoy what you can while you can—you're not going to let anyone give you rules? You can buy into the myth, you can buy into the misconception, or you can believe the truth.

Let's look at Job one more time. In chapter 12, his friends are trying to apologize for God. They are trying to protect His reputation. They are afraid that all Job's suffering will make it look like God isn't in control. They try to explain God. They keep talking and talking. "It must be your fault—you must be a sinner. It must be your doctrine. It must be this or that, because we couldn't believe in a God Who lets things like this happen under His watch."

Job looks at them and says, "No doubt you are people (in other words, you're not God), and your wisdom is going to die with you." He rebukes them for trying to tell lies and for trying to protect the honor of God. He says, "Listen, everybody can see it. It's obviously God." Verses 9 and 10 say, "Who among all these does not know That the hand of the LORD has done this, In whose hand is the life of every living thing, And the breath of all mankind?"

Job is saying, "Hey, wait a minute. You're trying to give excuses for God. Everybody knows the hand of God is in this." He didn't feel like he had to apologize for God. He didn't have to explain God. God is God, and we are not.

People today try to explain God. They give excuses. He did certain things. But do we ever just take God at His Word? Do we ever say, "If that's Who God says He is, I'm OK with that"?

We sometimes try to reconcile things with our little finite minds, our little limited brains. We try to match up what we understand with something in the mind of God, which is infinite, which has no limits. Job, though, decided to trust God and not try to explain it.

In chapter 13, Job says, "Hold your peace with me, and let me speak, Then let come on me what may! Why do I take my flesh in my teeth, And put my life in my hands? Though He slay me, yet will I trust Him. Even so, I will defend my own ways before Him." Job looks at his friends, looks at his wife, and says, "That's it. No more talking, no more explanations, no more anything. He can kill me, but I'm still going to trust Him. It doesn't matter. Whatever He does, I'm still going to trust Him."

Job understood the big picture of God. He knew God was loving and just and in control. Job didn't try to explain why his suffering was happening. He just accepted that it was happening and kept looking at Who he knew God was. Job was saying that he couldn't explain God, and these people were still misrepresenting Him, but he was going to trust Him.

Job didn't take a blind leap; his faith started with what he knew from his personal relationship with God. He chose to believe in what he had already discovered. It's the same for us. The way you and I can understand what God's Word is saying is by a personal relationship with the Creator of the universe. It will not be because we blindly step off the cliff. It will be because we have a personal relationship with God, and because we choose to trust Who God has told us He is.

Job knew he had a personal relationship with God, and he knew in his heart there was more going on than could be seen. His journey toward being able to trust God and being able to have His perspective began long before the tough times came. He pursued a relationship with God, and all his understanding and righteousness followed.

His journey started with a step of faith. Will you trust God today?

WHERE WAS GOD WHEN...?

This is one of the most difficult questions many Christians face. The Millennial Generation is asking this question with more urgency than any generation before it. This book and DVD series will answer these 'Why' questions in the same way God does in Scripture, with 'Who' answers - by focusing on the character and nature of God Himself. Tragedy and crises are not foreign concepts to students. From disappointment to terrorism, they are confronted with the "new norm" in the world today. For a generation that is tired of clichés, this study cuts through the noise and gets to the heart of the issue with biblical answers.

AVAILABLE AT WOLSTORE.ORG